THE TROUBLE-SHOOTING GUIDE TO CHRISTIAN EDUCATION

John R. Cionca

ACCENT BOOKS
Denver, Colorado

ACCENT BOOKS

12100 West Sixth Avenue
P.O. Box 15337
Denver, Colorado 80215

Copyright © 1986 Accent Publications
Printed in the United States of America

Library of Congress Catalog Card Number 85-73069

ISBN 0-89636-191-8

Second Printing

To

Dennis, Harold, Dick, Byron, Keith and Lew

Models and Mentors

ACKNOWLEDGMENTS

Sincere appreciation is given to the believers of Trinity Baptist Church, Mesa, Arizona, and Southwood Baptist Church, Woodbury, New Jersey, who have allowed me the privilege of fourteen years of ministry. My joy in service has been directly related to many co-workers who willingly carried the responsibility of teaching the timeless truths of the Scriptures.

I also want to acknowledge the invaluable assistance that Mrs. Barbara Hanrahan has given to me through the transcribing and finalizing of this manuscript.

Most importantly, I am grateful to my wife, Barbara, to my children, Ben and Betsy, and to our heavenly Father who has given us the joy of living together as a family.

PREFACE

For over a decade I worked as a specialist in the field of education. I ministered in three congregations, and worked as an educational consultant for several organizations. My full attention was given to playing my best as a team member of a ministry staff.

Six years ago I accepted the opportunity to be the manager of a team, a mid-sized, East Coast congregation. Before, I only had to play second base. Now, as senior pastor I found myself responsible for everything from catching to center field. I was still interested in Christian education, but now I also had to give supervision to missions, counseling, shepherding, stewardship and, obviously, to preaching.

Pastors and pastoral staff members are called to be leaders of a team. In the game of discipleship they cannot play all of the positions by themselves. They must be manager-coaches of others who will play the game. They share their leadership with assistant coaches who must be trained to develop the players. The teaching ministry of the local church is played well when the pastor, staff members, and program leaders manage well.

Although there are many comprehensive books that present the church's educational task in great detail, our leadership's daily ministry involvements do not afford them the time to find a place to retreat and study three to four hundred page books on the theology of Christian education, the Christian educational process, or even the administration of the Christian education program. Many of the pastors and pastoral staff with whom I fellowship share the same basic concerns:

—What program is right for my church?
—Where do I find enough teachers for Sunday School?

—How can we train people so that they become good teachers?

—What if we don't have enough money or adequate facilities for a good program?

The primary intent of *The Troubleshooting Guide* has not been to write a textbook for Christian education majors in seminary, although there is significant benefit to them in this volume. Rather, it has been to help practitioners already on the field, desiring an update and a better knowledge of C.E., who cannot afford the time to acquire it.

This book is intentionally small. Each chapter deals with a primary area of Christian education. The chapters themselves follow a question and answer format, giving practical answers to real issues. The design of the book will allow the busy church leader to pick it up, and then lay it down when necessary. Although there is a continuous flow of thought, the question and answer format allows adequate breaking points. In addition, the index at the back of the book provides easy access to questions on specific issues.

This book has been written for my colleagues who share in the teaching ministry of the local church. It is my hope that these suggestions will help pastors and lay leaders multiply their effectiveness in guiding their educational teams.

John R. Cionca, Ph.D.
Edina, Minnesota

CONTENTS

1

BUILDING A TEAM:
Staffing

When I was in the elementary grades, we could hardly wait for school to finish so we could get to the ball field. A quick snack at home, a few phone calls for recruitment, and we were on our way. Everyone in the neighborhood found a place on the team.

When I went out for high school baseball, the team was put together more selectively. Over two hundred fellows tried out, but after three cuts, less than thirty remained.

In professional sports, building a team is an art; scouting is ongoing and thorough; computer selection is a science; and fitting together a complement of players is a formidable task.

Our role as church leaders can be likened to the manager of a team. Our responsibility is not to play the whole game alone, even though the game is enjoyable and challenging, but to play well through the cooperative efforts of a team of players. Teaching the people of God the Word of God can only be done effectively when we use the skills of the whole team.

The answers to the questions which follow focus our attention on building a good educational team.

Why does staffing seem so difficult in many churches?

Staffing does not only *seem* to be a problem for churches, it is a chronic problem for most churches. There are a number of reasons why church programs are inadequately staffed.

First, the church experiences with its members what society at large is experiencing. Most Americans are spectators, not participants, and this attitude is prevalent in the church. Many come to church to "get something for themselves," perhaps a worship experience or a good Bible study. However, few have the attitude that they have come to serve others.

Second, although there are some individuals who have taught faithfully for several decades, the church's teaching staff is often composed of younger and middle-aged adults. Oftentimes the teachers are relatively new in Christ or new to the church. A church that has a large senior population, or one that rarely sees growth through new members, can expect to find staffing a problem.

Third, a simple reason for staffing problems is that a church is trying to offer too much program for its staffing capabilities.

A fourth reason for staffing difficulty that is often overlooked is the attractiveness of the existing program. If the church has a great worship service, if the pastor is a gifted Bible expositor, people are not eager to miss the service. If the adult Sunday School division is vibrant, educational, and a fun place to be, the adults will not want to give up that hour to serve in the three-year-old department.

Fifth, staffing is difficult when there exists a feeling that "only the gifted few" are able to teach. Many people do not think they have the "gift of teaching," and therefore figure that serving in the church's educational program must not be for them.

10

How do you find enough people to run a C.E. program?

As leaders in the church we have direct input on the magnitude of our church's program. If we want a full-blown evangelism program, an in-depth discipleship program, a complete music program with graded choirs and handbells, and a comprehensive Christian education program, then we must realize something may have to give. For some churches it might be amount of program, for others the quality of their program. The crucial element is that we must always seek a balance of programming. Where there is planned balance, it is possible not only to find enough people for the Christian education program, but also to have substitutes prepared.

Our starting point is to continually stress that a Christian is a server. The example of Jesus (Mark 10:45) teaches us that we should not seek to be ministered unto (warming a pew), but to minister to others. As team leaders we need to emphasize that it is not the special or unusual person who serves, but that it's the abnormal Christian who fails to follow his Lord in this matter.

A second attitude must also be cultivated. The word *teaching* terrifies many laymen. But many who may not feel they have the "gift of teaching," still enjoy children. Take the example of Jim. An engineer, Jim loved the Lord and children. Jim might not have responded to the title *teacher*, but he is glorifying God doing the same thing as an *educational worker*.

A third, but sometimes overlooked, point is that in a program which is completely staffed, there is no need to find enough people. Staffing involves recruitment and maintenance of staff. A church that enjoys good maintenance of staff will spend less time looking for new staff.

Here are some suggestions for discovering new workers:

● Survey the congregation with a "Serving Christ Together"

11

form. Two sample forms for recruitment are provided at the end of this chapter.

● Present the importance of serving during a new member-ship class. One class session should be dedicated to this.

● Look at people who are currently serving and consider if they could work in a higher level of responsibility.

● Use your teaching staff as a network of outreach for additional staff. Although recruitment should be done by program leaders, the regular workers can do a lot of P.R. work among their friends.

One last suggestion, avoid S.O.S. appeals in the bulletin to inform people of needed help. Notices such as, "We need four workers in our junior department immediately," negatively impact on the congregation. They tend to motivate by guilt, suggesting that any warm body will do, and communicate that the program is running poorly. No one wants to go down with a sinking ship.

Instead, focus on the positive. Enthusiastically highlight what's happening in various Sunday School departments. Recruit through personal contacts, and support your staff once they are recruited. The need to continually find educational workers will diminish with these efforts.

What is the ideal teacher like?

The literature on teacher competency reveals an ongoing controversy between whether there are inate *characteristics* of a good teacher, or if certain learned teaching *behaviors* are practiced by good teachers. Among noted characteristics, good teachers know their subject matter; they are pleasant and confident, and they esteem their students. Behaviorally, competent teachers individualize instruction, vary their methods, maintain a good classroom atmosphere, and teach for application. Whether we use characteristics or behaviors, there is probably no end to describing the ideal teacher.

As I have worked with people, I have become less impressed with their background and credentials, and more impressed with their attitudes and performance. What type of person would make a good educational worker? Although not original, I would want a F.A.T. person! Let me observe an individual who is *F*aithful, *A*vailable, and *T*eachable, and I'll show you a person who could work on the educational faculty of any church.

He may be a pipefitter or an executive; she may be a lawyer or a homemaker, but the faithful, available and teachable person who can follow a Sunday School quarterly or lesson plan, will be able to minister meaningfully to students.

Is there a certain amount of knowledge that a person should have before he is considered for teaching?

A friend of mine became a Christian when he was 26 years old. Immediately after becoming a Christian he was encouraged to get involved teaching Sunday School. The man began to teach a class of children, and each week he studied diligently to be adequately prepared for his kids. It was not unusual for him to call up the pastor's elementary-age daughter to figure out how to pronounce the names of certain Bible personalities or book titles. If you were to now ask Dr. Donald Orvis, seminary vice-president and professor, what helped him grow spiritually, he would include at the top of the list his early teaching experience where each Sunday he was just "one step ahead of the pack."

There is no certain amount of knowledge that a person should have before he is considered for teaching. If people have demonstrated that they are faithful, available and teachable, they should be trusted with the position, and then helped to become effective. The younger they are in Christ, the closer should be their supervision. With positive encouragement, the F.A.T. person will grow quickly in Bible knowledge and spiritual maturity.

What qualifications should I have for my teachers?

While some churches require their teachers to sign a statement that they'll not engage in the "dirty dozen," I feel comfortable listing these as qualifications for teachers:
- A born-again Christian with a desire to grow in godliness.
- A member of the church or in agreement with the church's doctrinal statement.
- One who nurtures his personal relationship with Jesus Christ through regular Bible study, prayer and personal worship.
- One who can commit the necessary time for personal preparation, staff meetings and shepherding of the students.
- One who supports the total church ministries of worship, teaching, missions, evangelism and stewardship.

How important are job descriptions?

I admire pastors who can generate policy and procedure manuals, and who with ease can spit out job descriptions for each church ministry. Although few people enjoy paper work, most of us recognize the importance of some of those printed pages.

Job descriptions have an essential place because they spell out for the worker the expectations for his or her ministry. Would you take a position in a church if you were approached in the following manner?

Leader: Would you be able to teach in our Sunday School?

Prospect: Well, what age group would you like me to teach?

Leader: Oh . . . we have several openings.

Prospect: What shall I teach them?

Leader: I'm not sure what materials we're using.

Prospect: How long am I expected to teach? Who would I go to if I had any problems?

Leader: Oh, that's not important right now; we could work something out later.

Even though there might be an occasional individual who would accept a position with that ambiguity, it is wrong for a leader to expect an individual to make a decision based on inadequate information.

Rather, we need to look closely at our needs, and then spell out those needs in simple, accurate expectations. With a specific job description, a person can give sincere consideration and prayer toward an opportunity. In addition, if the individual is married, he or she could share and receive input from the spouse.

What should be covered in a job description?

At least four ingredients should be detailed in a position description:

- Definition
- Relationships
- Specific Responsibilities
- Qualifications

The *definition* specifies that the person is a member of the teaching faculty with responsibility to a specific class or age, i.e., first graders, junior highers, library, etc.

The paragraph following *relationships* describes who appointed the worker for the position (usually the C.E. committee or the program director); who will be his immediate supervisor (the person to whom the worker can turn for help); and the tenure of the teaching assignment.

The *specific responsibilities* detail every aspect of what is expected of the worker. Nothing should be expected of the person unless it has been spelled out in this section.

Qualifications let the individual know that he is expected to walk closely with the Lord, and to be a team member in the overall ministry of the church.

A collection of job descriptions related to Christian education are given at the end of this chapter. Feel free to use the format, parts, or even whole descriptions where they apply to your church.

How long should a teacher be expected to serve?

It is important when recruiting to give the teacher a specific tenure of service. Resentment can build up in a person who has been serving faithfully, yet has never been asked if he wants a break or if he would like to relinquish that area of service. Even though a person should be encouraged to look at teaching as a long-term ministry, specific terms of service should still be presented. From the sample job descriptions you will notice that their normal length of service is one year, sometimes extending to two years for administrative positions. The twelve month term is realistic for several reasons:

- It allows workers enough time to adequately determine whether they are in a suitable area of ministry.
- It provides adequate time for them to be trained in that area of ministry.
- It recognizes that their personal and family situations may change over time.
- It lets them know that they have an option of terminating that area of service without a heavy guilt trip being placed upon them.

A One-Year Contract of Service can be signed by the teacher at the time of his first appointment and subsequent reappointments. Annual appointments to service can be staggered by quarters so that the terms of service do not expire at the same time for the entire educational faculty. Early childhood teachers might sign their annual contracts in March, children's workers in June, youth teachers and leaders each September, and the adult staff from December to December.

My experience has been that teachers who are regularly encouraged have been more than happy to serve many years. Some may want a short break from their responsibility; some may desire to work in a different area; but well cared-for teachers enjoy serving. See the sample "My Commitment to Service" contract at the end of the chapter.

Who should do the teacher recruitment?

Although who does the recruiting varies depending on the size of the church, in general each program leader should be responsible for the recruitment of workers within that program.

The Children's Club Director should recruit line leaders. The Sunday School superintendent or the department superintendents should recruit for their programs. The same procedures should be followed for the children's church, youth programs, and so on.

The Christian Education Committee and program leaders need to have good communication in order to avoid duplication of effort and the badgering of people. Each program leader needs to have a team concept because it is possible that as he presents the burden of junior high sponsorship, the person might reveal a greater desire to work with pre-schoolers. This name should be passed on to another leader.

A program leader who is sensitive in recruitment can motivate members, help other program leaders, and be assured of a fruitful ministry for the teacher placed in his own program.

How can we coordinate recruiting efforts?

Some churches use a form where people check all the areas in which they may be interested in ministering. Leaders of both the educational program and other church ministries should come together at least once a quarter to study these service forms. In addition, at these meetings they can review the church membership list and consider people who have recently joined the church.

In a smaller church the pastor often ends up being the clearinghouse for names. Nevertheless, there is a benefit in several people coming together to look at the possibilities. We each have biases, and may tend to subconsciously see a peron's name and assume he either is or is not a prospect. The quarterly meeting of ministry leaders will elicit more workers' names, and also coordinate the recruitment of those individuals.

Once again it should be stated that an individual who approaches a prospective teacher should be open to the possibility of the person serving in a different area of ministry. The senior high youth sponsor should not try to coerce someone into only working with the high schoolers. He should be very open to the desire of the person to ring in the handbell choir if that is the preference. There is no room for selfish attitudes when recruiting.

Also, contacts for teaching should never be made in the hallway or parking lot of the church. The old adage, "You get what you pay for," is true in recruitment. The more personal the contact, the more accurate picture of the task given, and the greater the excitement of the leader, the more likely will be a fruitful response on the part of the contact.

Program leaders should first telephone a prospective worker, seeking an appointment to meet with him or her to present the teaching opportunity. At their meeting the importance of the program should be explained. The specifics of the job discussed, and the support and resources for the worker described. The home meeting should conclude with prayer, and with the program leader promising to phone in one week to receive the prospective teacher's prayerful response.

If the prospect is willing to teach, materials are further explained, a contract is signed, and the new worker is asked to observe a few teachers prior to assuming the new responsibility.

If the person chooses not to make a commitment, the progam leader can discern if he or she would be willing to work as a substitute, or has interest in another area of ministry.

I keep recruiting people to teach, but many quit within a year. How can I stop this large turnover in staff?

There can be a number of reasons for failure to retain staff. Some that are common are listed below:

1. A program leader who is inadequate. Many programs experience a staff turnover because the superintendent or program leader is failing to do an adequate job. Perhaps the individual is negative and rarely encourages the workers. Perhaps he is dominant and always feels he has to have his way or push his own ideas. Maybe he is conspicuously absent and the teachers feel that they have been abandoned without a resource. Failure to remove an inadequate program leader will cause the self-removing of many staff.

2. A leader who is in child-bearing years. It is likely that those who are willing to teach in the early childhood and children's division are from the young married age group. When a Sunday School is staffed heavily with adults in their 20s and 30s, you can expect baby fever to occasionally remove people from teaching positions. Where teachers have had an enjoyable experience, however, they usually return to the classroom within a year after the arrival of the newest child.

3. Poor recruitment often results in the resignation of staff. Everything should be done up front to make sure that the person is faithful, available and teachable; that the job is clearly presented to him; and that he has had an opportunity to observe someone doing what is expected of him.

4. Recruiting on a rotation basis. Some churches, in order to plug their finger into the hole of the staffing dike, have made the

compromise of placing people in a short-term responsibility. Where staffing is on a quarterly, or even worse, a monthly basis, many people are used in a relatively short amount of time. These individuals may think they have done their duty, and that it is time for someone else to take a turn. They do not view the short-term service as an ongoing ministry. They have not had enough time to see the assignment as their ministry in the church.

5. Many workers feel inadequate and begin to question whether they have "the right stuff" for teaching. What they need is close, encouraging supervision by their program leader, and also some encouragement and praise from the pastor. One or two notes per year by the pastoral staff or program leader to an educational worker is a strong incentive for them to maintain their important responsibility.

It seems that every Sunday I get called by a teacher stating that he or she is sick or for some reason will not be able to teach. How do I handle these continual short-notice situations?

The two most common ways of handling these situations are to find a substitute for the class or to combine classes. Combining classes is not a bad idea where other classes are using the same curriculum, when facility space will allow for a larger group, and where the teacher can have additional materials ready so that each student will be personally involved with the lesson.

A better way to handle the absentee problem is to have *stand-by substitutes*. Some individuals can be recruited specifically as teaching substitutes. Part of their job description would state that they would only be expected to teach once a month.

A good group from which to recruit substitute teachers is the professional educators in your church. Most teachers have had their fill of teaching by the time Friday afternoon rolls around. Although they are the most skilled in teaching, they may not be the best Sunday School teachers. Many quite openly state they do not want anything to do with the teaching ministry of the church. Others feel a responsibility to use their gifts in the local church, but lack enthusiasm about their church classroom.

These professional educators are excellent substitutes. They can usually be notified on relatively short notice and still do a good job in the classroom. While their joy in service may come by serving on a committee or singing in the choir, they can still use their professional skills on an occasional basis to enhance the educational ministry of the church.

A second place to get substitute teachers is from that group of people who turned down the invitation to be a regular teacher. Program leaders will find some people hesitant to assume a weekly teaching responsibility (oftentimes for very valid reasons), but when given the opportunity to serve once a month at the most, they are willing to work.

Depending on the track record of each program's teachers, two or three substitutes per department or program should be adequate to handle absentee teachers.

The staff within my department do not get along with each other. What can I do to help them?

There can be many reasons why people do not get along. The more we can focus people's attention on our goals, rather than on others, the better off we will be. As we labor with all that is within us to present our students mature in Christ, we will grow in Christ, too. The staff members need to be gently encouraged to remember that God has made each one unique. Yet while there are differences in background, preferences and styles, the common goal of maturing our students in Christ remains the same. Where there is diversity within the staff, the program leader must be the blending agent to keep the team going in the same direction.

If a staff member is insensitive, unkind or outright obnoxious, the pastor or program leader can confront that person in love. That individual's problem is not with the other staff, but in his relationship with the Lord. Until that relationship with the Lord is made right, he will not be able to have an adequate relationship with the other staff members.

Occasionally, there will be a situation where it is best just to allow one or two staff members to move into another area of service. In one ministry I worked with a couple who was serving faithfully with our young people. When another couple joined them, however, things began to fall apart for both couples. After several meetings it became apparent that the couples would have difficulty working together.

We could have spent much time working with and forcing the situation. Instead, we began a new ministry at the church, and I asked the second couple to give leadership to that new endeavor.

Both programs are currently running well, and both couples feel they have a good ministry with their students. Although some may disagree with the idea of making staff changes because of differences, the bottom line is that people are different and some do not naturally work well with others. After all, that's why McDonald's sells Big Macs, Fish Sandwiches and Chicken McNuggets.

How do you remove a person from a job in which he is failing?

I have only known one person who felt he had the gift of confrontation. Needless to say,.this individual left a trail of scars and wounds among his congregation when he was asked to resign. If you're like me, you do not like confrontations, and therefore you tend to allow a person to stay in a job longer than he should.

Some people who are failing know they are not doing a good job, and they are open to suggestions. Your years in leadership have also told you, however, that there are some people who are ignorant of their failure, or stubbornly want to cling to a position for personal reasons. Where there is openness to change, training is the answer. Where there is resistance to change, or a consistent inability to fulfill job requirements, removal is the only answer.

As a pastor or as a program leader, I am out of place trying to remove a person if I have not had an ongoing relationship and close supervision with that worker. For example, I should not let things build and build until I simply want to remove the person from the position. Rather, as I see the early stages of failure, I should meet with that person to encourage him in those areas.

An appointment should be made by the worker's supervisor to review his or her job description. Such a review would serve as an opportunity to share areas of concern. If, after several sessions with the individual, it becomes apparent that the person cannot change or is unwilling to change, gently inform the person that at the end of the contractual period (one year) he needs to consider ministering in a different area. There may be one or two other areas of service in the church that you could suggest for him to consider.

Failure to remove an inadequate worker, especially a failing program leader, will lead to other staff withdrawing from ministry.

Do you have any suggestions for improving teacher attitudes?

My son has had four different teachers in his first three years of elementary school. Two of the teachers were relatively easy-going, they allowed for individual differences, and they were positive in their outlook. The other two teachers were more regimented and negative in their outlook.

With the positive teachers, our son had a growing enjoyment for school and a greater appreciation for himself. With the teachers who put "one wrong" in big red letters (rather than 49 right), or "this work is not neat," his work degenerated, and his self-esteem fell with it.

This same idea applies in the Sunday School. The best way to improve teacher attitudes is to personally maintain good attitudes about the teachers.

Here are some suggestions to help improve teacher attitudes. First, make a commitment yourself never to say anything critically harmful or negative about a third party. Second, recognize that the same commitment will not necessarily be made by others about you. Third, have a healthy view about the depravity of man and the transforming power of God. Fourth, model good, positive attitudes yourself. Fifth, keep your teachers' focus on the spiritual goals and larger vision, not on the petty problems of who took their markers.

The more we can help our teachers focus on the importance of Christ building His church, and the eternal consequences of our co-labor, the more likely they will follow the modeling of our positive attitudes.

How much communication do I need with my teachers?

Program leaders need a minimum of monthly communication, and perhaps as much as weekly visual contact with their teachers. Pastoral staff will have less direct exposure. Since most teachers do not expect the pastor or other staff members to be intimately involved with their classroom, any contacts that are made will enhance those relationships.

Educational leadership, even the senior pastor, can be involved in these types of communication builders:

- Attend a major training program where you personally take a moment to thank and affirm the teachers.
- Write a note of encouragement to each teacher annually.
- Call the teacher once or twice per year, asking them for one classroom related prayer request and one personal prayer request that you might remember in prayer.
- Where possible, sit in on a program or spend a few minutes with the staff during a department planning meeting.
- Regularly highlight in the church newsletter some aspect of the church's educational program.
- Praise the staff or use illustrations of their classroom success.
- Incorporate in the church calendar an annual teacher recognition banquet.
- Let them know in any expressible way, "I really care."

Summary

We are impressed when we watch a superstar make a big play. Yet the outcome of most ballgames does not depend on a solo performance, but on how well the whole team plays for the duration of the game.

In the game of Christian education we do not have one superstar. God's plan is to equip all the saints for the work of the ministry (Ephesians 4:12). Even if we had a very talented worker, it would be unfair to him to expect him to play several positions. It would also be unfair to others who would be deprived of the enjoyment of the game and the opportunity to use their skills.

Most of us will probably never use a computer to draft our educational players. But with sensitivity to the leading of the Holy Spirit and with thoughtful team building principles, we can serve our churches well as managers and coaches.

SERVING CHRIST TOGETHER

Name _____ Phone _____ Date _____

Every member of the body of Christ is important for the growth and maturity of our people. We have each been gifted to serve (I Corinthians 12). We have each been empowered to serve (Acts 1:9); and we have each been commanded to look for ways to serve (Galatians 6:10). We ask that this questionnaire be answered by every member and friend who wants to share in our service for Christ. Please check those activities in which you are willing to help; or to continue helping for the coming year; or about which you would like more information before deciding to help:

( ) Administration
( ) Records or Accounting
( ) Sunday School Teacher (age preferred: ____)
( ) Sunday School Substitute (age preferred: ____)
( ) Vacation Bible School Staff
( ) Children's Church
( ) Christian Club Program
( ) Puppet Ministry
( ) Youth Work, Leadership or Sponsor
( ) Greeting Visitors
( ) First-Time Visitation
( ) Evangelistic and Follow-up Visitation
( ) Hospital Visitation
( ) Occasionally Provide Refreshments
( ) Occasionally Open Home for Meetings
( ) Occasionally Provide Overnight Housing
( ) Provide Occasional Transportation
( ) Home Bible Study Leader
( ) Telephoning
( ) Maintenance of Church Building (specify type) ____
( ) Maintenance of Church Grounds (specify type) ____
( ) Other Ideas

( ) Provide Occasional Office Help
( ) Women's Ministries
( ) Men's Ministries
( ) Counseling
( ) Directing Children's Choir
( ) Musical Instrument: ____
( ) Choir Member
( ) Solo or Ensemble Singing
( ) Community Involvement
( ) Library Check-out/Worker
( ) Audio-Visual Work
( ) Art Work and Promotion
( ) Special Education Ministries (Deaf, Physically Handicapped, Mentally Handicapped)
( ) Nursery Care
( ) Ushering
( ) Communion Preparation
( ) Kitchen

28

INTEREST AND SKILLS SURVEY

For just as we have many members in one body and all the members do not have the same function, so we, who are many, are one body in Christ, and individually members one of another. And since we have gifts that differ according to the grace given to us, let each exercise them accordingly.

Romans 12:4-6a (NASB)

Jesus Christ is the Lord and Head of His Church and each believer is a UNIQUE and VITAL part of this Body. God has a ministry for each of us and we will not be spiritually or humanly fulfilled if we are not active in the ministry for which God has equipped and intended us. This is both a privilege and a basic responsibility we have as God's children. Ministry is a many peopled thing!

Here in _____ Church you have an almost unlimited opportunity for fellowship and meaningful involvement. Our purpose is to "honor God by equipping people to disciple the nations."

This survey is intended to help our staff better coordinate the total ministry of Christ through the entire body of believers and to assist you in finding and enjoying your place of ministry.

We ask that you carefully complete this survey in its entirety and return it.

If you have any questions, please ask Pastors _____, _____, or _____.

WE NEED EACH OTHER

BUILDING A TEAM:

DATE _____

NAME _____ Phone _____ Work _____

Address _____ Zip _____

Occupation _____ Male _____ Female _____

AGE GROUP OR CLASS: _____

Single _____   Married _____   Church Member _____

Listed below are various areas of ministry, each preceded by four boxes:

If you have ever served or participated in the area of activity in this or any other church, please check the box headed PAST.

If you are presently involved in the area of activity in this church, please check the box headed PRESENT.

If you would be willing to become involved in a listed activity here with us, please check the box headed FUTURE.

If you wish to become involved but need training to do so, in addition to checking the FUTURE box, *also* check the box headed TRAINING.

M I N I S T R I E S

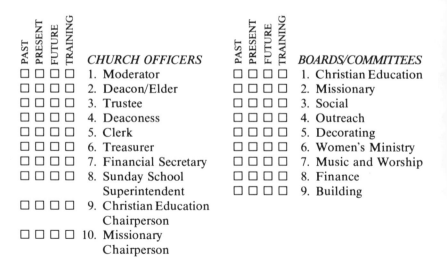

PAST	PRESENT	FUTURE	TRAINING	*CHURCH OFFICERS*
☐	☐	☐	☐	1. Moderator
☐	☐	☐	☐	2. Deacon/Elder
☐	☐	☐	☐	3. Trustee
☐	☐	☐	☐	4. Deaconess
☐	☐	☐	☐	5. Clerk
☐	☐	☐	☐	6. Treasurer
☐	☐	☐	☐	7. Financial Secretary
☐	☐	☐	☐	8. Sunday School Superintendent
☐	☐	☐	☐	9. Christian Education Chairperson
☐	☐	☐	☐	10. Missionary Chairperson

PAST	PRESENT	FUTURE	TRAINING	*BOARDS/COMMITTEES*
☐	☐	☐	☐	1. Christian Education
☐	☐	☐	☐	2. Missionary
☐	☐	☐	☐	3. Social
☐	☐	☐	☐	4. Outreach
☐	☐	☐	☐	5. Decorating
☐	☐	☐	☐	6. Women's Ministry
☐	☐	☐	☐	7. Music and Worship
☐	☐	☐	☐	8. Finance
☐	☐	☐	☐	9. Building

PAST	PRESENT	FUTURE	TRAINING	
				GENERAL CHURCH MINISTRY
☐	☐	☐	☐	1. Head Usher
☐	☐	☐	☐	2. Usher
☐	☐	☐	☐	3. Greeter
☐	☐	☐	☐	4. Host/Hostess

CHRISTIAN EDUCATION MINISTRIES

PAST	PRESENT	FUTURE	TRAINING	
				CRADLE ROLL DEPARTMENT (0-2 years)
☐	☐	☐	☐	1. Cradle Roll Director
☐	☐	☐	☐	2. Cradle Roll Committee
☐	☐	☐	☐	3. Cradle Roll Worker
☐	☐	☐	☐	4. Cradle Roll Outreach
				EARLY CHILDHOOD (2-6 years)
☐	☐	☐	☐	1. Coordinator
☐	☐	☐	☐	2. S.S. Department Superintendent
☐	☐	☐	☐	3. S.S. Teacher
☐	☐	☐	☐	4. Children's Club Director
☐	☐	☐	☐	5. Children's Club Worker
☐	☐	☐	☐	6. Children's Church
☐	☐	☐	☐	7. Substitute Teacher
				CHILDREN'S DIVISION (Grades 1-6)
☐	☐	☐	☐	1. Coordinator
☐	☐	☐	☐	2. S.S. Department Superintendent
☐	☐	☐	☐	3. S.S. Teacher
☐	☐	☐	☐	4. Missionary Education Teacher

PAST	PRESENT	FUTURE	TRAINING	
☐	☐	☐	☐	5. Children's Club Director
☐	☐	☐	☐	6. Children's Club Worker
☐	☐	☐	☐	7. Children's Church
☐	☐	☐	☐	8. Substitute Teacher
				YOUTH
☐	☐	☐	☐	1. Coordinator
☐	☐	☐	☐	2. S.S. Department Superintendent
☐	☐	☐	☐	3. S.S. Teacher
☐	☐	☐	☐	4. Discipler
☐	☐	☐	☐	5. Sponsor
☐	☐	☐	☐	6. Retreat Helper
☐	☐	☐	☐	7. Substitute Teacher
				ADULT DEPARTMENT
☐	☐	☐	☐	1. Coordinator
☐	☐	☐	☐	2. S.S. Department Superintendent
☐	☐	☐	☐	3. S.S. Teacher
☐	☐	☐	☐	4. Substitute Teacher
☐	☐	☐	☐	5. Growth Group Participant
☐	☐	☐	☐	6. Home Bible Study
☐	☐	☐	☐	7. Discipleship Group Leader
☐	☐	☐	☐	8. Growth Group Leader
☐	☐	☐	☐	9. Class Officer
				GENERAL
☐	☐	☐	☐	1. Sunday School Secretary
☐	☐	☐	☐	2. S.S. Department Secretary
☐	☐	☐	☐	3. Pianist

31

BUILDING A TEAM:

PAST	PRESENT	FUTURE	TRAINING	CHRISTIAN EDUCATION MINISTRIES, *continued*
☐	☐	☐	☐	4. Librarian
☐	☐	☐	☐	5. Children's Librarian
☐	☐	☐	☐	6. Library Assistant
☐	☐	☐	☐	7. Audio Visual Worker
☐	☐	☐	☐	8. Vacation Bible School Director
☐	☐	☐	☐	9. V.B.S. Teacher
☐	☐	☐	☐	10. V.B.S. Secretary
☐	☐	☐	☐	11. V.B.S.Craft Leader
☐	☐	☐	☐	12. Backyard Bible Clubs
☐	☐	☐	☐	13. Summer Camp Ministries
☐	☐	☐	☐	14. Camp Counselor
☐	☐	☐	☐	15. Family Camp— Leadership
☐	☐	☐	☐	16. Family Camp— Helper

MUSIC MINISTRIES

PAST	PRESENT	FUTURE	TRAINING	
☐	☐	☐	☐	1. Organist
☐	☐	☐	☐	2. Pianist
☐	☐	☐	☐	3. Choir Member
				☐ Soprano
				☐ Alto
				☐ Tenor
				☐ Bass
☐	☐	☐	☐	4. Instrumental Soloist Instruments played _____
☐	☐	☐	☐	5. Instrumental Ensemble
☐	☐	☐	☐	6. Vocal Soloist

PAST	PRESENT	FUTURE	TRAINING	MUSIC MINISTRIES, *continued*
☐	☐	☐	☐	7. Vocal Ensemble
☐	☐	☐	☐	8. Children's Choir Leader
☐	☐	☐	☐	9. Youth Choir Leader
☐	☐	☐	☐	10. Worship Leader
☐	☐	☐	☐	11. Handbell Choir Member
☐	☐	☐	☐	12. Handbell Choir Leader

OUTREACH MINISTRIES

PAST	PRESENT	FUTURE	TRAINING	
☐	☐	☐	☐	1. Hospitality for Groups
☐	☐	☐	☐	2. Discussion Leader for Bible Studies
☐	☐	☐	☐	3. Church-wide Outreach Events
☐	☐	☐	☐	4. Men's Outreach Events
☐	☐	☐	☐	5. Women's Outreach Events
☐	☐	☐	☐	6. Investigative Bible Studies
☐	☐	☐	☐	7. Visitation
☐	☐	☐	☐	8. Senior Citizen's Ministry
☐	☐	☐	☐	9. Shut-in Ministry
☐	☐	☐	☐	10. Jail/Prison Ministry
☐	☐	☐	☐	11. Hospitality for ☐ Youth ☐ Adults
☐	☐	☐	☐	12. Hospitality (Unexpected) Overnight/Meals
☐	☐	☐	☐	13. Hospitality (Expected) Overnight/Meals

PAST	PRESENT	FUTURE	TRAINING	
				COMMUNITY CONCERNS
☐	☐	☐	☐	1. International Students
☐	☐	☐	☐	2. Tutoring
☐	☐	☐	☐	3. Nursing Home Visitor
☐	☐	☐	☐	4. Food/Clothing—Poor
☐	☐	☐	☐	5. Literature Distribution
☐	☐	☐	☐	6. Handicapped Ministries
☐	☐	☐	☐	7. Rescue Mission Work
☐	☐	☐	☐	8. Other

_____

PAST	PRESENT	FUTURE	TRAINING	
				PROPERTY AND MAINTENANCE
☐	☐	☐	☐	1. Air Conditioning/Heating
☐	☐	☐	☐	2. Automotive/Bus/Van
☐	☐	☐	☐	3. Carpentry/Cabinet Work
☐	☐	☐	☐	4. Cement Work/Masonry
☐	☐	☐	☐	5. Cleaning/Custodial
☐	☐	☐	☐	6. Electrical
☐	☐	☐	☐	7. Flooring/Carpet
☐	☐	☐	☐	8. Glass
☐	☐	☐	☐	9. Handyman
☐	☐	☐	☐	10. Insurance
☐	☐	☐	☐	11. Real Estate
☐	☐	☐	☐	12. Interior Decorating
☐	☐	☐	☐	13. Landscaping/Gardening

PAST	PRESENT	FUTURE	TRAINING	
				PROPERTY AND MAINTENANCE, continued
☐	☐	☐	☐	14. Painting
☐	☐	☐	☐	15. Wallpapering
☐	☐	☐	☐	16. Plumbing
☐	☐	☐	☐	17. Roofing/Ceiling
☐	☐	☐	☐	18. Snow Removal
☐	☐	☐	☐	19. Other (specify)

_____

_____

PAST	PRESENT	FUTURE	TRAINING	
				SPECIAL INTEREST MINISTRIES
☐	☐	☐	☐	1. Arts/Crafts
☐	☐	☐	☐	2. Athletic Coach (specify sport)
☐	☐	☐	☐	3. Athlete (specify sport) ___ ___
☐	☐	☐	☐	4. Lifeguarding
☐	☐	☐	☐	5. Bulletin Boards/Displays
☐	☐	☐	☐	6. Commercial Art
☐	☐	☐	☐	7. Cooking
☐	☐	☐	☐	8. Kitchen Worker
☐	☐	☐	☐	9. Drama
☐	☐	☐	☐	10. Puppetry/Ventriloquism
☐	☐	☐	☐	11. Lighting Effects
☐	☐	☐	☐	12. Audio/Electronics
☐	☐	☐	☐	13. Radio/Television
☐	☐	☐	☐	14. Tape Ministry
☐	☐	☐	☐	15. Projectionist
☐	☐	☐	☐	16. Photography
☐	☐	☐	☐	17. Driving Church Vehicle

PAST	PRESENT	FUTURE	TRAINING	*SPECIAL INTEREST MINISTRIES, continued*	PAST	PRESENT	FUTURE	TRAINING	
☐	☐	☐	☐	18. Flower Arranging	☐	☐	☐	☐	25. Computer/Word Processor
☐	☐	☐	☐	19. Journalism/ Writing/Editing					
☐	☐	☐	☐	20. Printing	☐	☐	☐	☐	26. Office Mailing
☐	☐	☐	☐	21. Public Relations/ Publicity	☐	☐	☐	☐	27. Office Records
					☐	☐	☐	☐	28. Office Typing
☐	☐	☐	☐	22. Sewing	☐	☐	☐	☐	29. Office General Clerical
☐	☐	☐	☐	23. Medical ☐ Doctor ☐ Nurse ☐ First Aid ☐ CPR	☐	☐	☐	☐	30. Prayer Ministry
					☐	☐	☐	☐	31. Prayer Chairperson
☐	☐	☐	☐	24. Accounting/ Bookkeeper	☐	☐	☐	☐	32. Prayer Breakfast

MISCELLANEOUS INFORMATION

1. Are you willing to donate blood for emergencies?

      YES   NO   MAYBE

2. Do you speak any foreign languages?   YES   NO
   (specify language) _____

If you have a talent or ability not mentioned here, or a ministry which you feel we should get involved in, please write it below.

_____
_____
_____

SUNDAY SCHOOL SUPERINTENDENT

DEFINITION: The Sunday School Superintendent is a member of the educational faculty of the church with the general administrative responsibility of the entire Sunday School.

RELATIONSHIPS:
1. Responsible to the Christian Education Committee.
2. Responsible to the Pastor.
3. Appointed for a two year term of service beginning in January.

SPECIFIC RESPONSIBILITIES:
1. Supervise the ministries of the department superintendents.
2. Be a resource person to the department superintendents and to the teaching staff.
3. Work with the Christian Education Committee in providing annual training for the workers.
4. Be sure that each department has monthly unit planning sessions.
5. Maintain an inventory of current curriculum.
6. Six weeks before each quarter, make sure the office has a list of new curriculum to be ordered.
7. Assist department leaders with names for potential new workers.
8. Build fellowship and morale among the workers.
9. Supervise the mini-shepherding and follow-up of the various departments.
10. Promote the Sunday School within the church.
11. Represent the Sunday School to the Christian Education Committee.
12. Work with other program leaders to coordinate the entire educational program of the church.

QUALIFICATIONS:
1. A born again Christian with a desire to grow in godliness through personal Bible study and prayer.
2. Member of the church.

35

SUNDAY SCHOOL SUPERINTENDENT, *continued*

3. Gifts and abilities in the area of educational leadership.
4. A burden for improving the quality of our Christian education.
5. Demonstrated ability to work with people, commanding authority yet treating them with respect.
6. Support the total church program of worship, eduation, fellowship, missions and stewardship.

Job Description

EARLY CHILDHOOD COORDINATOR

DEFINITION: The Early Childhood Coordinator shall be an administrative leader on the educational faculty of the church, and shall serve in ministry with children aged two years six months through Kindergarten.

RELATIONSHIPS:

1. Responsible to the Christian Education Committee.
2. Responsible to the Minister of Christian Education.
3. Appointed for one year term of service beginning in _____.

SPECIFIC RESPONSIBILITIES:

1. Observe, evaluate, coordinate and give oversight to the Sunday morning educational activities within the Early Childhood division.
2. Be a resource person to whom workers in the division may come for materials, equipment or help with children.
3. Recruit teachers and workers necessary for the program functions.
4. Conduct divisional planning meetings.
5. Instruct new workers; offer counsel and guidance to all workers.
6. Provide substitutes as needed.

EARLY CHILDHOOD COORDINATOR, *continued*

7. Encourage follow-up; keep accurate records.
8. Evaluate the effectiveness of the program and the educational workers.
9. Handle emergencies.
10. Develop a list of curriculum needed and submit to church office six weeks in advance of a new quarter.
11. Encourage teachers to attend conferences, conventions and other training opportunities.

QUALIFICATIONS:

1. A born again Christian with a desire to grow in godliness through personal Bible study and prayer.
2. Member of our church.
3. Educational leadership ability and gifts.
4. Demonstrated ability to understand and work with young children and adults.
5. Desire to improve the quality of Christian Education.
6. Support the total church program of stewardship, worship, missions, fellowship and education.

Job Description

CHILDREN'S DIVISION TEACHER

DEFINITION: A Children's Division teacher shall be a member of the church's educational faculty, assigned to ministry with a class of children in grades one through six.

RELATIONSHIPS:

1. Responsible to the Christian Education Committee and the Children's Division Coordinator.
2. Appointed for a one year term as noted in the teacher contract.

37

CHILDREN'S DIVISION TEACHER, *continued*

SPECIFIC RESPONSIBILITIES:
1. Weekly lesson preparation.
2. Knowledge of the children with attention to developmental characteristics and everyday life situations.
3. Consistent attendance at each division planning meeting.
4. Punctual attendance at the place of duty (arriving 15 minutes prior to starting time).
5. Follow-up of absentees through a phone call, note or visit.
6. Teaching as a team member of a department, using methods which encourage student self-discovery.
7. Willingness to share in personal and departmental training and evaluation for improvement of the learning process.

QUALIFICATIONS:
1. A born again Christian with a desire to grow in godliness through personal Bible study and prayer.
2. A member of our church.
3. One who can commit the necessary time to personal preparation, staff meetings and shepherding of the students.
4. Support the total church program of worship, missions, stewardship, fellowship and education.

Job Description

CRIB NURSERY ATTENDANT

DEFINITION: The Nursery Attendant is a paid or volunteer member of the church educational faculty with specific ministry to infants of crib and creeping age.

RELATIONSHIPS:
1. The Nursery Attendant shall be directly responsible to the Director of Early Childhood Ministries and ultimately

CRIB NURSERY ATTENDANT, *continued*

responsible to the Christian Education Committee. The attendant will be appointed for a one year term (March—March) by the Christian Education Committee.

SPECIFIC RESPONSIBILITIES:

1. Arrive 30 minutes prior to regular or specially scheduled services and ascertain that the nursery is in a state of readiness to receive infants.
2. Supervise the reception and identification of infants and their supplies as they arrive at the nursery.
3. Ascertain, as nearly as possible, that only WELL babies are admitted to the nursery.
4. Comfort those infants who register unhappiness or discomfort by crying.
5. Make frequent and periodic checks for soiled or wet diapers and change them as they occur.
6. Give bottles and/or other nourishment as directed by and provided by the parents.
7. Maintain a state of personal cleanliness and appearance that will effectively diminish the inadvertent transmission of possible infections from one infant to another and to impart confidence to the parents.
8. Make a final check of all diapers near the end of each scheduled service to make certain the infants are returned to their parents clean and dry.
9. Make sure all bottles and other pieces of equipment are returned to proper parents.
10. Put nursery back in order in preparation for the next usage.
11. Be responsible for maintaining an adequate supply of fresh, clean linen.
12. Give adequate advance notice of expected absence to permit substitute staffing.
13. Keep Director of Early Childhood Ministries and/or the Christian Education Committe informed of the needs of the nursery.

CRIB NURSERY ATTENDANT, *continued*

QUALIFICATIONS:
1. A born again Christian with a desire to grow in godliness through personal Bible study and prayer.
2. In good general health.
3. A negative chest x-ray annually.
4. Capable of carrying out responsibilities.

Job Description

1st AND 2nd GRADE DEPARTMENT LEADER

DEFINITION: The 1st and 2nd Grade Department Leader shall be a member of the educational faculty and shall have specific responsibility in the administration of 1st and 2nd grade Sunday School.

RELATIONSHIPS:
1. Responsible to the Christian Education Committee.
2. Responsible to the Director of Childhood Ministries.
3. Appointed for a one year term of service beginning June 1 of each year.

SPECIFIC RESPONSIBILITIES:
1. Be aware of potential teachers and workers who may be recommended to the Director of Childhood Ministries for recruitment.
2. Be sure that each teacher and worker within each department understands the nature of his task.
3. Serve as a supervisor and resource person for each unit of teaching.
4. Conduct unit planning meetings in preparation for each unit of teaching.
5. Encourage teachers to actively participate in teacher training program.

1st AND 2nd GRADE DEPARTMENT LEADER, *continued*

> 6. Make sure supplies and materials needed for teaching are available to the teachers either in the department or general office supply.
> 7. Encourage workers to participate in church-wide projects.
> 8. Maintain adequate records for follow-up purposes.
> 9. Supervise the class report forms for absentee follow-up, assuring that each teacher has made proper weekly contacts.
> 10. Be sympathetic and cooperate with other areas of ministry within the church.

QUALIFICATIONS:
> 1. A born again Christian with a desire to grow in godliness through personal Bible study and prayer.
> 2. Member of the church.
> 3. Gifts and abilities in the area of educational leadership.
> 4. A burden for improving the quality of our Christian education.
> 5. Ability to work with people, commanding authority yet treating them with respect.
> 6. Support the total church program of worship, education, fellowship, missions and stewardship.

Job Description

CHILDREN'S CLUB LEADER

DEFINITION: A Children's Club Leader shall be an adult member of the church educational faculty, and shall work in club ministry with children in grades three through eight.

RELATIONSHIPS:
> 1. Responsible to the Christian Education Committee and the Children's Club Director.

CHILDREN'S CLUB LEADER, *continued*
2. Appointed for a one year term of service.
3. Work as a team member with other club leaders.

SPECIFIC RESPONSIBILITIES:
1. Assume responsibility of club members on his team, giving direction, assisting with Scripture memorization and following the guidelines in the club manual.
2. Follow-up on team members with visits or phone calls.
3. Participate in training sessions.
4. Assist in planning outside activities and be in attendance at them.
5. Dress appropriately.
6. Attend regular club planning sessions as scheduled by the Director.
7. Participate in each club meeting, arriving at the place of duty 15 minutes prior to club time.
8. Set a personal example for the children through participation, Scripture memorization and enthusiasm for the club.

QUALIFICATIONS:
1. A member of our church or in agreement with church doctrine and ministry.
2. A born again Christian with evidence of spiritual commitment.
3. An exemplary life of spiritual discipline.
4. An enthusiasm for club work.
5. Support the total church program of stewardship, missions, fellowship, worship and education.

Job Description

YOUTH ADVISOR

DEFINITION: A youth advisor is an adult member of the church educational faculty who serves specifically in the ministry

YOUTH ADVISOR, *continued*

of junior high or senior high young people. The youth advisor will work on a team of advisors who serve as "coaches and guides" for the young people. He or she should seek to work with young people, not running their program but helping them with their own ministry.

RELATIONSHIPS:
1. Responsible to the Youth Pastor.
2. Responsible to the Youth Coordinator of the Christian Education Committee.
3. Appointed for a one year term of service (September—September) by the Christian Education Committee.

SPECIFIC RESPONSIBILITIES:
1. To work with the Youth Pastor and young people in the planning of a balanced youth program.
2. To be friendly and personally interested in each young person, yet a mature adult to whom they can come for counsel. (Remember, you are not a teenager and kids do not expect you to be one.)
3. To supervise personally one program each month.
4. To attend social activities for your respective youth group. (This can be worked on a shared or rotation basis with other advisors.)
5. To assist the Youth Pastor in other matters pertaining to the youth ministry.

QUALIFICATIONS:
1. A born again Christian with a demonstrated evidence of spiritual commitment.
2. A member of our church.
3. One who nurtures his or her personal relationship with Jesus Christ through regular Bible study, prayer and personal worship.
4. One who can commit the necessary time for personal preparation, staff meetings and shepherding of the young people.
5. One who supports the total church ministries of worship, teaching, missions, evangelism and stewardship.

ADULT HOST

DEFINITION: The greeter shall be an active member of a particular group within the Sunday School, and shall welcome and give assistance to other adults within the class fellowship.

RELATIONSHIPS:
1. Responsible to the class leader.
2. Support the class leader in encouraging fellowship and interest among the group.
3. Support the teacher in the educational process.

SPECIFIC RESPONSIBILITIES:
1. On a regular basis, remain available in the church foyer before Sunday School to encourage visitors and non-attending members to attend the Sunday School class.
2. Offer assistance to anyone needing class information or accommodation for children.
3. Maintain a friendly, cheerful and warm demeanor in welcoming others.
4. Encourage participation in Sunday School.

QUALIFICATIONS:
1. Personal commitment to God and a love for people.
2. Member of our church.
3. High commitment to and participation in Sunday School and class activities.
4. Support the total church program of stewardship, worship, missions, fellowship and education.

COORDINATOR OF WOMEN'S MINISTRIES

DEFINITION: The Coordinator of Women's Ministries shall be a member

COORDINATOR OF WOMEN'S MINISTRIES, *continued*

of the church's educational ministry and shall be responsible for the church's overall program to women.

RELATIONSHIPS:
1. Responsible to the Christian Education Committee.
2. Appointed for a one year term of service.
3. Work with other leaders to meet the various needs of women.

SPECIFIC RESPONSIBILITIES:
1. Plan Home Bible Studies for women as needed, recruiting teachers and providing study materials.
2. Give oversight to special craft activities as requested.
3. Plan and give oversight to ministry opportunities.
4. Plan and give direction to one special event for women each year.
5. Prepare and submit a budget each year by November 1.
6. Meet with the Christian Education Committee twice yearly.

QUALIFICATIONS:
1. A born again Christian with evidence of spiritual maturity.
2. A member of our church.
3. One who nurtures her relationship with Christ through prayer, Bible study and personal worship.
4. Support the total church ministry of worship, missions, stewardship, fellowship and education.

Job Description

HOME BIBLE STUDY LEADER

DEFINITION: A Home Bible Study Leader shall be a member of the church's educational faculty, involved in weekly Bible study ministry with adults.

HOME BIBLE STUDY LEADER, *continued*

RELATIONSHIPS:
1. Responsible to the Christian Education Committee and the Senior Pastor.
2. Appointed for a one year term of service.
3. Work in coordination with the elders and Sunday School class leaders regarding any special needs which may arise.

SPECIFIC RESPONSIBILITIES:
1. Regular Bible Study preparation.
2. Maintain regular studies by establishing time and location for meetings.
3. Guide discussion of the assigned lesson; encourage sharing and participation by all.
4. Encourage prayer for and instruction among group members.
5. Encourage participation in outreach projects selected by the group.
6. Make arrangements for substitutes or changes in location as necessary.

QUALIFICATIONS:
1. A born again Christian with evidence of spiritual maturity.
2. A member of our church.
3. One who nurtures his relationship with Christ through prayer, Bible study and personal worship.
4. Support the total church ministry of stewardship, fellowship, missions, worship and education.

MY COMMITMENT TO SERVE

One Year Ministry Appointment

I hereby receive from the Christian Education Committee an appointment to serve my Lord and Savior, Jesus Christ, as

_____

from _____, 19____, until _____, 19____, at which time I may consider reappointment for another year.

As a worker in the educational program of the church, I will:

1. Give of my best in the service I have accepted. I understand that it is not exceptional ability nor outstanding qualifications, but faithfulness to my assigned task that is of supreme importance.
2. Regularly attend the planning meetings of my department or organization.
3. Remember at all times that I am working with the lives of individuals to help mold them after the life of the Son of God as set forth in the Word of God.
4. Attempt to lead in public and in private a life which is exemplary, honoring my Lord as well as having the best possible influence upon those I lead.
5. Support the total church program of worship, education, fellowship, missions, stewardship and evangelism.
6. Affirm the statement of belief established by our church fellowship.

Therefore, my beloved brethren, be ye stedfast, unmoveable, always abounding in the work of the Lord, forasmuch as ye know that your labour is not in vain in the Lord.

I Corinthians 15:58

On behalf of the Christian Education Committee: Dated _____

_____, Chairman

_____, Ministry Director

_____, Teacher

2

KEEPING THE TEAM GOING: Organization

Several times each season Barb, Ben, Betsy and I go to watch the Philadelphia Phillies play baseball. We use on-the-street parking a few blocks away, and then hustle up to the 700 section behind first base. The inexpensive seating allows us to indulge in a few extra treats. My kids aren't into peanuts, but the ice cream vendor draws their attention every game.

While we are watching nine men play ball on the field, it's easy to forget all the organization which takes place behind the scenes to keep a baseball team going. Occasionally we hear something about "the front office" or "the management making a trade." We rarely recognize the administration needed for ticket sales, parking, uniform laundering, grounds maintenance, media publicity, player contracts, and the other details necessary to keep a team running smoothly. Without good organization, a team can never become a winner.

The ministry of the church of Jesus Christ is eternally more important than a baseball game. But if good structure is necessary for secular enterprises, it is imperative for the educational program of the local church.

Is the Christian Education Committee really necessary?

You've probably heard the old saying: "A camel is a horse that a committee put together." Because of the ineffectiveness of some groups, there exists an eagerness to do away with committees, or at least by-pass them somehow. A committee should not be a group of uninformed, disjointed individuals, but rather a team of coaches who give guidance and supervision to their players.

The Christian Education Committee is a group of individuals who are appointed to give oversight to all aspects of the church's educational ministry. In some churches the committees meet often and assume heavy responsibilities, including the selection of staff, the scheduling of special meetings and the planning of programs such as Vacation Bible School. Other committees meet less frequently for the purpose of communication by program leaders.

The teaching ministry of the church is so important that it necessitates close oversight. Even in a church where there is a Christian Education minister or paid program leaders, a Christian Education Committee still helps coordinate the various programs. "How much program should our church have?" "How can we best divide our students for learning?" "What materials should we use?" All are questions that can be answered by the Education Committee.

The committee should not try to reinvent the wheel on every issue, nor control every situation. Rather, their function is to maintain a current appraisal of the educational program, giving special attention to needs which may arise. Many of the decisions of the Christian Education Committee can be implemented directly. Where facilities are concerned, they may need to work with a board of trustees. Where major policies are of concern, they may want to consult the official church board.

The Christian Education Committee can also be a safeguard and sounding board. Let's say, for example, your club leader wants to take your clubbers to see the play "Annie." Some parents may be bothered by that activity. Your club leader, children's church worker, or youth advisor can be safeguarded from criticism by running their programs through the Christian Education Committee.

A first baseman is usually only concerned with playing his position well. In the same manner, the left fielder is primarily concerned with the outfield. The Christian Education Committee serves as the manager and coach of the educational team, giving oversight to the ministry and making sure all the workers and programs are pulling together smoothly.

Who should serve on the Christian Education Committee?

There are two ways that Christian Education Committees are usually formed. Some congregations vote or appoint individuals at large. These individuals are not necessarily related to any given program, but are interested in Christian education in general. This type of organization is useful for evaluating the various programs and functioning as a sounding board for program leaders. Since the people usually appointed to this type of committee are a random sample of the congregation, their input is usually a good gauge of how the congregation is responding to the various programs.

The second way of forming the Christian Education Committee is to comprise it of the various program leaders. For example, one committee may be composed of six members including the Sunday School superintendent, a youth sponsor, a boys club leader, a girls club leader, a training hour director and a board chairman. This type of committee works well in the areas of planning and coordinating. Each committee member can share what is happening in his or her own area, and can also ask for input on specific concerns. This structure is convenient for coordinating and scheduling activities well in advance. These dates can be placed on the church's master calendar for coordination with other programs.

Before you formulate the committee, determine if its primary purpose is evaluation/guidance or if it is coordination. Who should serve on the committee will be answered by the primary function of the committee.

What types of items should be on the C.E. agenda?

Any item that is of educational concern can be placed on the agenda. A few words of warning should be given, however. No one needs extra meetings. If quarterly meetings are sufficient, do not schedule monthly meetings. Keep meetings to the agenda; honor the time of your volunteers.

We also need to remember that people work the programs, not committees. Program leaders ought to be given freedom in developing their area of ministry. The committee should be an encouraging resource to the worker, serving to coordinate his or her efforts with others.

Items that are commonly on the agenda of the Christian Education Committee are:

- Prayer
- Reports on program by program leaders
- Review and evaluation of curriculum
- Appointments to service
- Evaluation of programs

- Scheduling of activities (i.e., VBS; Sunday School picnic; training seminars; annual recognition banquet)
- Adoption of policies (usually initiated by a program leader)
- Developing an annual educational budget

What should be included in our Christian education budget?

Although some C.E. budgets are divided by age divisions, a more typical Christian Education budget may look like this:

Sunday School	2400
Youth Ministries	1600
Women's Ministries	500
Vacation Bible School	750
Library	500
Children's Club—girls	200
Children's Club—boys	200
Other C.E. Programs	500
Christian Education Materials	400
Training	1500
Audio-Visual Equipment	500

The amount placed in each category of the budget should honestly reflect the program needs. Obviously, every program could use additional money, but the committee must look both at what it wants to accomplish and what it can afford. Programs that receive club member dues can have less in the budget. Sunday Schools that use take-home papers and student books will need to reflect those costs. The committee should plan well in advance what type of summer programs or training opportunities it envisions. The budget will then be adequate to provide those ministries.

Unfortunately, like our federal government's budget, our church budgets have many fixed categories. Since churches must pay their pastors, the mortgage company, utilities and so on, it is the program area of the church that is expected to be flexible. In addition, when a church has a high commitment to missions, a tight inflationary year may be especially hard on a program budget.

Our boards and committees must be helped to understand that while bricks and mortar are important, they can never be more important than the training of our teaching staff, and the purchasing of materials that will aid in the study of God's Word. Our purpose is not the building, but the changing of lives that takes place within the building. Pastors, especially, need to lead the way in making sure that Christian Education budgets are healthy.

Should we have a Christian Education Organization Chart?

Whether you have a chart or not, you probably already have an organization. Although there may be some individuals who are unsure of who their immediate supervisor is, or how they relate to others, most workers know where they fit into the program.

The advantage of having an organization chart is that it gives you a visual picture of the overall Christian Education program. A chart can let you know, for instance, how much ministry you have for junior highers in comparison to senior citizens. It can show if you are understaffed and where the greatest staffing needs are. For example, some charts are designed with room in each box for both the position title (i.e., guide, superintendent, sponsor, teacher) and the worker's last name. By looking at the chart it is easy to tell which programs have adequate staff, and which programs have a staffing need.

The organization chart should be constructed with flexibility built-in, allowing names to be added or deleted as changes are made. A chart can be drawn on a large sheet of posterboard and then covered with plastic. A wooden molding can be placed around the chart to dress it up and to attach it to the wall.

A Dyno labeler can be used to print program and staff names. For example, programs could be listed in blue; leaders' positions labeled in red, and the names of the workers printed in black. As you add additional C. E. programs, or as you make staff changes, the sticky labels can be easily peeled off the plastic. The cardboad chart itself would not be damaged with the many changes.

What does departmentalization mean?

Departmentalization is a term used to describe a way of breaking down into manageable units a Sunday School or other Christian Education program. A small church may have only four or five departments consisting of young children, elementary age children, youth and adults. In a larger church you may find the elementary children's division depart-mentalized into primaries (grades 1-2), middlers (grades 3-4), and juniors (grades 5-6), or even a department for each grade.

A department is not the same thing as a class. Within each department there might be two to four classes. All students within one department usually study the same curriculum. The teachers of a department may group the students differently for various learning activities.

This systematic division of people into more manageably sized groups also establishes reasonable spans of control for the superintendents working in leadership.

What is the best way to organize the children's program?

In many large churches an individual is given the position of Children's Coordinator. It is not unusual in these situations to see programs for children organized by age stratification. The programs for 1st and 2nd graders, 3rd and 4th graders, and 5th and 6th graders would be planned and conducted specifically for each group of children.

A more workable solution for most churches, however, is to organize first by program. Most educational leaders function best when they have a specific program for which they are responsible. For example, the children's division can be organized with the subdivisions of Sunday School, children's church, club programs, training programs, and so on. Each program would have a coordinator, and then within each program there could be a further breakdown, for example, by age groupings.

How large should a teacher's class be?

If Johnny, Billy and Sam are in the same class, it may already be too big for one teacher. Several factors affect how many students can be grouped for learning:
- Number of volunteers available for teaching
- The experience and competence of the teacher(s)
- The number of students in a given grade
- The nature of the students
- The teaching objectives—can they be reached in a larger group?
- Shepherding expectations—how many students can be followed up?

Recognizing individual differences within teachers, and even individual differences within classes (eight six-year-old boys will be different than eight six-year-old girls), let me nevertheless make some general recommendations:

- Young children (two through kindergarten): One teacher for every five students
- Elementary children (grades 1—6): One teacher for every six to eight students
- Youth (junior high, senior high): One teacher for every ten students
- Adult: One teacher for every 20—30 students, with discussion leaders selected when the class is broken down into small groups.

Larger classes or groupings are possible for some learning activities. For example, the senior high mid-week study may have two team-teachers leading 18 students. In general, however, appropriate methodology and manageable shepherding encourages the ratios above.

Should our adults be age-graded, or should we use electives?

The adult Sunday School is usually divided into elective classes or age groupings. Sometimes adults are allowed to divide themselves by selecting which teacher they prefer. Some larger churches try to combine both ways, by having fellowship groups begin the hour, and then allowing adults to regroup according to elective choice.

On the surface it might appear that one system is superior to the other. For example, one might think that new Christians would benefit from an elective program which would allow them to study basic Christianity, rather than the minor prophets. However, someone else might argue that the best way for a young Christian to grow is to put him in a class with other Christians in the same stage in life, and he will learn with and from them regardless of the subject.

Some important questions which may be overlooked when making a decision on the adult format are: "How are fellowship and shepherding provided in the local congregation? How are visitors assimilated into the church? How does the church keep track of, and care for its adults?"

A church where the deacons maintain shepherding responsibilities for smaller fellowship groups, would probably benefit from elective classes in the Sunday School. Offering a variety of topics for study can best reach the differences in students' backgrounds and interests.

On the other hand, a church that is having difficulty keeping in touch with the needs of its people, and desires to improve its fellowship and outreach, may benefit from an adult structure based on stages of life. A class of young marrieds can study Philippians, but they can also plan baby showers, and visit other young marrieds who are new to the church.

Our priorities must be to have quality teaching no matter what the format, and to provide a balanced ministry to adults. The Christian Education Committee should work with other committees to make sure the adults of the church have opportunities for both cross-age fellowship, as well as fellowship and study within their own age groups.

How can we coordinate the Christian Education program with other church programs?

Some churches have a vehicle for coordination through an official board or church council that receives input from various committees. Even where a unified board exists, it is still beneficial to have the leaders who are involved in education, worship, fellowship and evangelism meet at least twice a year for prayer, planning and other necessary communication.

Every church should also have a master calendar in the church office. Individuals, groups or committees can submit their programs or dates to the official board or through the church office as a clearinghouse. Remember, communication is a two-way street. For the sake of committee planning and communication, early notification of events should also be sent from the church office to the committee chairmen and program leaders. This will not only let the left hand know what the right hand is doing, but will also encourage a team concept where all involved realize that they are working together in the ministry of Christ. What each one does impinges on others.

How can we increase attendance in our program?

Some churches have annual Sunday School contests to motivate their people to reach out to others. Some members spend Saturdays inviting children to ride the bus to Sunday School the next morning. Some departments or classes have special incentives for students who bring visitors. All these emphases can be used sincerely to build enthusiasm and keep the growth of the Sunday School before a congregation. And, each of these principles also apply to the morning worship service and all other church programs.

The first step in increasing a Sunday School's attendance is to have a good Sunday School. You've sat in classes, and I've sat in classes, that are so poor that only an extreme commitment to Christ will enable the person to endure week after week. While some people have that kind of commitment, the average person will only attend programs that are enjoyable, Biblical and personally relevant. When these qualities characterize our program, attendance is likely to increase even with limited promotion.

Improving the quality of a program is 80 percent of the battle. The remaining 20 percent is motivating people to have the attitude, "we want to let others know what they're missing." The best salesperson is a satisfied customer. Our folks need to know that our programs are open to visitors, and that their friends would not be embarrassed if they came. Extra Bibles should be available in the classroom. In addition, teachers of all ages need to be sensitive to the Biblical illiteracy and difficulty in reading experienced by many who attend their classes.

Rally days and occasional attendance contests have their place, but the most consistent method for increase is to have our people possess the attitude: "This is a great place to learn what God says about life. You would really enjoy and benefit from this program. Why don't you come with me next Sunday?"

What should be the pastor's involvement in the Christian Education program?

Because the pastor has many demands on his time, he cannot have an in-depth involvement with every church program. He has responsibilities to Christian education, worship, music, community outreach and stewardship matters. He must also divide his time between church administration, sermon preparation, visitation and counseling. But even with the limited time the pastor has, he can still demonstrate a visible involvement with the Christian education program.

His involvement should not be as administrative head of any specific program. That level of responsibility must be handled by a person who can give it the necessary leadership and time. He can best assist the educational ministry through his team building and encouragement of the teaching staff. He may offer suggestions for recruiting or counsel the C.E. Committee, but his relationship with the workers themselves is of most importance.

His personal joy in service, and his appreciation and encouragement of the teachers is a good blend of involvement.

What type of records should be kept?

The best answer to this question is, "Whatever records you will *use*." Some churches maintain a detailed file of enrollment and visitors. Where an adequate outreach ministry exists, these names can provide good contacts for a deeper commitment. There is little benefit, however, of having records of people who are not interested in the church.

Many churches design their program so that each teacher is a shepherd of a mini-flock within the congregation. In this arrangement each teacher maintains his or her own records. Names of visitors who come to the class, or another church program, may be given to a teacher for follow-up. If, in time, the individual shows little interest, the name is not retained in the records of the teacher or department. If they demonstrate an interest, they are added to the mini-flock responsibility of the teacher. For the purpose of overall coordination, names of students should be kept by the teacher/shepherd, and also by the department coordinator or church office.

Regardless of how classes are structured, statistics should be kept for each program, and for the classes within the program. These records are useful for evaluation and planning. The attendance figures can give you the age proportions of your congregation, the involvement of your congregational members in various programs, and growth trends by program.

Attendance statistics can also give you a basis for making room assignments. Adequate square footage can be planned according to the number of learners and student needs. Statistics will also be helpful as you plan for growth and the future division of classes.

How large should our church be before we hire a Director of Christian Education?

There are many variables involved when it comes to the expansion of church staff. Churches vary in per capita giving. They also vary in amount of mortgage indebtedness or monies committed to missions. All of these factors must be considered in determining the feasibility of pastoral staff expansion.

Some churches wait until they reach 200 or 250 before they add the second staff person. Others seek to add the second pastoral staff at the 150 mark, hoping his ministry will generate the growth expansion necessary to support his salary.

A general rule of thumb is that a staff person can be added to a church for every 100-150 regular attenders. Since this figure would also include support staff such as secretaries or custodians, others have followed the ratio of one pastoral staff for every 150-200 congregants. These generalizations are usually based on the number of people needed to support the new staff and the expanded program.

Churches differ in the expertise of the laity within their congregations. One church may have great musicians, with good lay choir directors or worship leaders. Another congregation may have people with administrative or educational backgrounds, who effectively coordinate parts of the C.E. program. Other congregations may have a team of youth sponsors who provide an excellent, balanced youth ministry. Whether a church hires a Director of Christian Education, an Associate Pastor, a Youth Pastor, or a combination of these positions, will also be determined by variables in the local congregation.

A smaller church that is expanding to a second, full-time pastor will likely need to call an individual who can wear two hats. The leadership must recognize he will not be able to wear both hats equally well, but since the pastor is already wearing several hats, two hats aren't that bad.

A competent Minister of Christian Education will, in a short time, produce a program which will attract additional singles and families. In a world that tries to lure people away from Christ, a strong Christian education and youth ministry is greatly sought by parents. Unless a church has a lay person who could oversee a strong Christian education program, I would heartily encourage the calling of the second pastoral staff with Christian education responsibilities in his job description.

Do you need a Sunday School Superintendent if you have a Director of Christian Education?

A Sunday School Superintendent is concerned with the overall administration of the Bible school. If a church has a Director of Christian Education, and if that church does not have many C.E. programs, the Director could probably also serve as the Sunday School Superintendent.

A church that is able to afford a D.C.E., however, probably has an educational ministry comprised of several programs. This multi-dimensional program will necessitate the Director of Christian Education serving as an administrator and resource person to the educational faculty as a whole. If this is the case, it is best that the position of Sunday School Superintendent be filled so that one person can still give specific leadership to that major program.

Some churches utilize divisional coordinators for the Sunday School (pre-school, children, youth, and adult) who work directly under the D.C.E. Where the area of responsibility for the Minister of Christian Education is not too large, this arrangement can be profitable. Where there are four or more educational programs, however, the educational pastor will probably want to lead the Sunday School through the single representation of the Superintendent.

What exactly is the function of the Minister of Christian Education? What is his relationship to the lay program leaders?

The basic job of the Director of Christian Education should be that of encouraging, coordinating, counseling, and doing everything possible to help the leaders, teachers and members of the church serve through teaching. As a professional member of the pastoral staff, this person is also charged with the Biblical responsibility of "equipping the saints for the work of the ministry." He serves the congregation best in the role of a faithful and trustworthy counselor and administrator to the lay leaders and groups who are responsible for the church's educational program.

More specifically, the Education Minister will work with the Christian Education Committee in developing educational aims and policies, coordinating the educational program, promoting the educational program, staffing and training those who will serve in the program, and evaluating each program's effectiveness. A sample job description for the Minister of Christian Education is provided on the following page.

Summary

We live in an orderly universe. From a wristwatch to an automobile, there is organization based on design and purpose. As managers and coaches of an educational team, we are charged with the task of "maturing the saints for the work of the ministry." That commission necessitates organization. If good organization is of concern to Xerox and AT&T; if it is necessary for every successful ball team in our country, then it is of much more importance to the local church, the body of Christ.

Job Description

MINISTER OF CHRISTIAN EDUCATION

DEFINITION: The Minister of Christian Education shall be a full-time member of the pastoral staff who serves as administrator of the church's educational ministries.

RELATIONSHIPS:
1. The Minister of Christian Education shall be responsible to the Board of Deacons, and shall work directly under the supervision of the Senior Pastor.

SPECIFIC RESPONSIBILITIES:
1. Give administrative leadership to the total educational program of the church.
2. Assume supervisory responsibilities, working as a leader and guide to all program leaders. He shall be available to counsel teachers, officers, youth leaders and superintendents.
3. Work with program leaders in regular evaluation and improvement of the educational ministries.
4. Serve as an ex-officio member of the Christian Education Committee, utilizing program leaders' suggestions in the development of educational goals, policies, curricula and programs.

MINISTER OF CHRISTIAN EDUCATION, *continued*

5. Train and assist program leaders in the recruitment and training of new workers.
6. Minister as a team member of the pastoral staff, promoting Christian education, yet understanding the importance of the whole ministry of the church.
7. Serve as a resource person to all personnel of the teaching staff, therefore keeping informed of educational techniques, materials and programs through private study, personal associations and professional conferences.

QUALIFICATIONS:

1. A mature, born again believer who has displayed a love for the Lord, a call to ministry, and effective service in the church.
2. A student of the Bible, with professional training in Christian education.
3. Ability to work with people, commanding authority yet treating people with respect.
4. Supportive of the total church program of stewardship, worship, missions, fellowship, education and evangelism.

3

STUDYING THE GAME: Program

Last summer our family vacationed in Vermont. The main reason for traveling north was to visit some good friends who were working there during the summer. Jack is the manager of the Vermont Reds, the double A team of Cincinnati. During the day we played tennis, swam, and enjoyed renewing our friendship. Each evening we traveled to the ballpark to cheer for the team.

Whether you view baseball from box seats or from a television, there are certain fundamentals of the game that never change. An inning consists of six outs, three outs per team. There are nine regular innings per game. The pitcher is the one who puts the ball in play. If the batter hits the ball, it must be caught in the air or thrown to a base to force out the runner.

The game of baseball is a composite of pitching, catching, fielding, throwing and batting. When we appreciate an exciting game, we realize that it is because the various parts of the contest were executed well.

As we look at the Christian education program in a local

church, we also see a composite of activities that, when played well, produce an effective outcome. When the components of Sunday School, youth groups, children's church and Bible studies are effective, the overall program will produce knowledge and maturity in Christ Jesus.

How do we develop a quality Christian Education program?

The Christian Education program is a ministry which seeks to teach and train people to be mirror images of Jesus Christ. In "teaching them to observe all that I have commanded you" (Matthew 28:20), each congregation could use a variety of ways to accomplish that divinely ordained function of the church.

Building quality into any program begins first with *attitude*. Quality can only come if those involved in the administration and teaching believe that they are involved in the most important task in the world. The Sunday School is not another program like Indian Guides, Girl Scouts or the 4-H Club. While Little League and piano lessons are important, the most essential time during the week are those hours when we learn more about God. A high view of our task will produce a high quality in the task.

The quality of the program is also directly related to the *leadership and teaching staff* within the program. The type of people we recruit, the effectiveness of our training, the ongoing communication and appreciation that we give, all contribute to the quality of our program. These concerns have been emphasized in the chapter, "Building the Team," and will be discussed further in the chapter, "Making the Team a Winner."

The amount of program will also affect the quality of the program. While is is important to offer diversity and balance, offering more program than you can staff will hurt the overall quality of the educational program. It is best when one new program is begun at a time, so that proper supervision and assessment can be given to assure the best possible quality.

Good organization, trained staff and even the learning environment (facilities), all have bearing on the quality of the Christian Education program. A quality program keeps regular attenders interested, and it is also the most important ingredient for outreach and growth.

How much program should we have?

Many pastors feel their church needs to be a full service church. When people look for a congregation, they look for one that has ministries for their family as a whole, as well as for the individual family members. Because of this, there is a tendency to try to offer more program than can be properly staffed and run. Realistic priorities, and an understanding of the congregation, will help church leadership determine how much program they should have.

First, the nature of the congregation determines program. Program is a means to an end. A program is begun for senior citizens, junior highers, or the deaf only if a church can reach out to those populations. A study of the population and sub-populations of the congregation itself should be taken into consideration when determining amount of program.

Some programs, such as the Sunday School, have a flexibility which makes them beneficial to churches of every size. A small congregation could have a Sunday School with only four divisions, whereas a larger Sunday School might have separate classes or departments divided by age or subjects. Other ministries, such as prison visitation, puppets or handbells, are affected by size and age-groupings. How many programs a church will provide must be related to the needs of the congregation and the sub-populations of the congregation.

Second, the number of available volunteers affects the size of program. The Christian education ministry of the church is just one of many programs within the church. A congregation may have a large home Bible study ministry, a multi-group music ministry or a comprehensive evangelism and discipleship program. A church cannot have more program than it can staff, so obviously the pastor and leadership must consider both the needs of their congregation and the direction in which they want to take the congregation.

In many churches the Sunday School seems to be declining. Why is this?

While some churches are experiencing Sunday School decline, this is not a universal situation. In fact, many churches have dynamic Sunday Schools that are growing annually. However, several factors may foster a decrease in Sunday School attendance:

1. The general decrease in church attendance both in number of attenders and increasing absenteeism among members.

2. A change in the purpose of the Sunday School. A number of years ago evangelism and education were the two main reasons for having a Sunday School. Many schools today have education and fellowship as their main purposes. While fellowship is essential, a de-emphasis of outreach will show a corresponding de-emphasis in attendance.

3. A maturing population. The primary attendees of Sunday Schools have traditionally been children, and now our fastest

growing populations are the older adults and young adults. Churches that do not have a population of children and middle adults will have difficulty building attendance.

4. A de-emphasis on busing to reach neighborhood children. The gas crunch in the mid 70s and the questioning of the long-term effectiveness of busing has led many churches to discontinue this outreach.

5. The development of full service churches. Many churches have provided additional programs for young people and a diversity of programs for adults. Many adults would prefer to attend a two hour Thursday evening home Bible study than the fifty-minute Sunday School. The home Bible study is usually in a more relaxed atmosphere and offers an opportunity for questions and personal interaction. Sunday School may be larger, more threatening and more structured. It is not that one program is better than the other, it's the simple fact that where students have several programs from which to choose, all of the programs do not maintain the same height of interest.

How can we build a healthy Sunday School?

Why is it that many fans support a professional team one year, yet do not attend the next season? Why are the facilities of some teams packed out, while other stadiums are empty? There is a direct correlation between what is happening on the field and the number of fans in the bleachers. People enjoy a winning team and avoid a losing team. A healthy team wins. It accomplishes its purpose.

A healthy Sunday School is one that is accomplishing its designed purposes. Most Sunday Schools have a primary focus on teaching the Scriptures, and a healthy Sunday School is one in which the teaching-learning process is being consistently accomplished. If fellowship is part of the Sunday School's purpose, then a healthy Sunday School is one which provides for fellowship. If outreach is part of the function of a church's Bible school, then it is healthy if it is seeing additions through its outreach efforts.

A healthy Sunday School needs a balance in curriculum, an adequate staff that enjoys its teaching ministry, and a learning atmosphere that facilitates spiritual growth.

To build health into a Sunday School, both attitudes and behaviors have to be monitored. Leaders and teachers need to have positive attitudes and a joyful understanding of their teaching privilege. This inner attitude will help generate better teaching. Equally important, leaders and teachers need to focus on teaching behaviors that encourage learning. As a teacher practices good teaching methods, his or her attitude will also improve. As the staff develops healthy attitudes and healthy teaching behaviors, those who attend the Sunday School will pick up on this positive influence, and the Sunday School as a whole will grow in quality.

What are the pros and cons of a children's church?

A children's church is usually a program for preschoolers and/or elementary age children that simulates an adult worship service at the child's own level. Many churches conduct the program during the worship service.

Some churchmen are opposed to separating children from parents during worship. Worship is caught as well as taught, and therefore the modeling of older brothers and sisters, friends and parents in a worship service is important. However, others question the relative value of a first grader sitting through a typical worship service compared to his participation in a program designed especially for him.

There is a danger in keeping children totally separated from the adult worship until they reach the youth years. It is during the junior high years that young people may not want to go to church, and are testing their own autonomy on their parents. If they have never been in an adult worship service until these years, the transition may be very difficult for them, and subsequently a point of conflict within the home.

It is beneficial for children to participate in adult worship, yet it is also advantageous for them to have a program at their own conceptual level. To accomplish both of these goals, some churches have what is called a *release time* feature of their worship service. For example, families may sit together in worship for the first thirty minutes of the service (thus allowing the children to share in the hymn singing, Scripture readings and special music), then just prior to the message the children are released for a thirty-minute program tailored to their learning level.

The release time emphasis has some drawbacks. For example, using sanctuary seating for only half of the service can be a problem in crowded worship services. The opportunities both for involvement in adult worship and learning at one's own age level must be carefully weighed in the individual congregation.

Other churches maintain a separate children's church for the morning service and encourage the inclusion of the elementary age children in evening worship services.

The format of the children's church varies among congregations. Some churches use a Church Time curriculum from a publishing house. Others may use that time for Bible memorization or missionary stories. A growing trend seems to be utilizing that time for a children's choir ministry.

Children's churches are primarily beneficial for children in grades one through four, although some churches extend it through grade six. If a release time schedule is followed, or if the children's church does not meet during the summer months, children have an opportunity for continuing contact with adult worship to learn the hymns of the faith and the forms of worship.

Is a mid-week program essential for our church?

The Scripture tells us not to forsake the assembling of ourselves together, but we are not told how often we should meet. We see the necessity to congregate for the purposes of worship, study and fellowship, but how often to meet or what forms our scheduled meetings should take is left to local congregations to decide.

Living in a post-Christian environment, it is difficult to maintain fellowship with other believers and a sense of camaraderie in Christ if we meet only on Sundays. Adults need additional fellowship during the week and our children and youth, who are under heavy peer pressure, also need more frequent contact with godly influences.

Whether a mid-week program is a Wednesday family night at the church, or decentralized home Bible studies and youth fellowships, each will vary from congregation to congregation. To accomplish its purposes, one church may choose to have a family night where a nursery is provided for young children, club programs for children, teenage studies for the young people, and electives or centralized meetings for adults. Another congregation may choose to have a program for children after school during the week, with studies for youth and adults during the evening. Again, it is important to have more programming than that offered each Lord's day, but the form of those programs may vary.

Since the family is so pulled apart throughout the week, many prefer a mid-week centralized program for the whole family. If space permits, all the groups can meet on or near the church campus on a Wednesday or Thursday evening. A two-hour program would allow children's programs to have recreation, a lesson, memorization, craft, etc., and it would also allow adults time for elective classes or home Bible studies near the church campus.

How does music fit into the Christian education program?

Music is an excellent vehicle for accomplishing many of the purposes of the church. For example, we can worship through music, teach and learn through music, fellowship with music and even present evangelistic messages through the medium of music.

Music can be used effectively in the Christian education program for teaching Biblical truths. It can also be used to allow a group of individuals to minister to another group of people. Repetitious and catchy tunes can teach everything from theology to Christian living. A group of kids who have learned some songs can also minister with that music to the congregation, residents of a nursing home, or other groups of young people.

If a church has a graded music ministry, this medium would take a lower profile in the Christian education program. Where there are not several choirs for children and youth, a portion of the educational programs should incorporate music as a method. A children's choir as a release-time feature of a morning worship service or a Wednesday program can be a good blend of Christian education and music. For example, kids can be taught the fruit of the Spirit by learning "The Music

Machine," and they can then minister to the congregation by sharing that musical.

Some T.V. commercials are easily memorized because they are repetitive, and they utilize a catchy melody. Both secular competition and the Scriptures themselves illustrate the importance of music in our teaching.

Should home Bible studies be related to the church? If so, how do I maintain accountability?

Those who affirm the doctrine of the priesthood of believers recognize that any group of two, five or eight believers has the freedom to gather and study the Scriptures. If home Bible studies exist in a church, their relationship to the church necessitates clarification.

If the church leadership initiates the home Bible study, then the church should exert some authority and control over it. For example, if the Bible study is promoted through the bulletin, and the group members are placed together by the pastor, then the pastor and the church should maintain control over leaders and curriculum. If the study is initiated by an individual or group of people, then the leadership cannot expect to have control, but neither should the study expect church promotion. Individual class home Bible studies may be sanctioned by the church but promoted only among members of the Sunday School class.

Accountability of home Bible studies is maintained by keeping up-to-date on the progress of each group. The person responsible for supervising the Bible study ministry should meet with the Bible study leaders on a weekly or bi-weekly basis. The meeting could be used for training, as well as updating what is happening in the lives of the various people attending studies.

Home Bible studies are very beneficial to the growth and life of a church. Some form of accountability and direction of the studies is essential, however, for coordinating that ministry with the overall church program.

I would like to begin a couple of small Bible studies in my church, but I'm afraid that it will hurt the attendance in prayer meeting. Might this happen?

Very few people have the time available to attend both mid-week service and a home Bible study. Even if a person were able to give Sunday evening, Wednesday evening and another evening to the church, is that a wise investment of time?

Our people are responsible for serving, for caring for their families, for jobs, for ministering to neighbors, and for personal rest. If a person is to maintain these different responsibilities, it is unlikely that he can be involved in both a mid-week prayer meeting and a home Bible study.

I began a home Bible study program in one church, and many people thought I had sold prayer meeting down the river. Attendance at the mid-week service did drop from an average of twenty-five to about fifteen people per week. On the surface it looked like there was a loss. But a deeper look revealed just the opposite. Whereas twenty-five people had been meeting each week for study and prayer, with the addition of five home Bible studies over one hundred adults were meeting weekly to examine the Scriptures and pray. Overall mid-week study of the Bible actually increased from 12 to 50 percent.

A comprehensive home Bible study program may lessen the Wednesday evening attendance, but offering both a Wednesday evening service and home Bible studies will reach additional families who would not normally attend one or the other.

We are thinking of starting a home Bible study or two. What are the advantages of a men's only or a women's only study versus a study for all adults?

My observation of Bible studies in various churches has led me to conclude that both men's or women's groups, as well as mixed groups have a place in church programming. Spiritual growth among group members may take place more rapidly in a same sex group. Some men are uncomfortable and more reserved in answering questions or praying aloud in a mixed group, than when they are in a small group of men. Women sometimes sense the same freedom when they are able to share their concerns in an all women's Bible study.

Also, men's Bible studies and women's Bible studies may be able to reach out evangelistically with greater ease. A couple may be attracted to a couples' study, but usually the interest of the husband and wife are not at the same level. The study may be an early morning Bible study or a noon study for men, a Thursday morning mother's-day-out study for women, or an evening study for either group, but the result will be a rich fellowship and growing spiritual life.

However, a couples Bible study guarantees one night of the week where mom and dad get a babysitter and go out together for a couple of hours. In many cases the couples will prepare their lessons together, and this encourages additional shared time. While a heterosexual group may jell more slowly, and may take more time for some individuals to open up, there are many rewards to men and women studying the Scriptures together. The different viewpoints often generate new and deeper insights into Scripture.

One of our biggest enemies today is the clock. Everybody has more things on their "to do list" than can reasonably be accomplished. When there is overcommitment and the family is being pulled in many directions, there is a great advantage also to mixed Bible studies. This is especially true of adult singles whose need to grow spiritually is sometimes matched by their need for deeper Christian fellowship.

Do you suggest groups of mixed backgrounds for Bible study?

Whether we're talking of men's groups, women's groups or mixed groups, there are advantages to having diversity within the group. Since the body of Christ has many members, yet one body, so, too, a good group would have both mature Christians and newer Christians. It would have young adults, middle adults and older adults. It would have couples as well as singles.

Single adults need mixed fellowship. If they have children, their children need contact with other opposite sex role models. The younger Christian needs to model after the more mature Christian. Younger couples need the fellowship of godly older couples. Diversity within home Bible studies not only prevents cliques, but it also opens our eyes to the larger family of God.

Our Vacation Bible School does not seem to have any long term results as far as assimilating neighborhood kids into our church. Do you have any suggestions?

It is not unusual for churches to follow up their VBS students with phone calls or letters, simply to find only a few returning to the Sunday School. We are glad for the one or two weeks of Bible study that we can share with our neighborhood children, but we also desire to minister to these families on a long term basis.

Usually the Vacation Bible School follow-up is from the teacher or pastor to the child. This may be the least fruitful type of follow-up. A better arrangement for follow-up is to first have the teacher or leader personally contact the adults in the family to let them know you appreciated having their children in the school. A cordial invitation to Sunday School can follow. Second, VBS students and their parents who normally attend church should reach out to the children. Peers can more easily recruit their friends.

More specifically, the class teacher can visit each home subsequent to the VBS with a brochure of the church and a description of the church's ministries. Not only can they share with the parents what is available for their child, but they can also mention church programs or resources that would be attractive to the adult. A letter to the entire family would be beneficial only if this personal, visible contact were first made.

Some churches have a fall, interdepartment Sunday School contest or a special Sunday School outing to follow-up on friends who came earlier in the summer for Vacation Bible School.

Sadly, even if we assimilate some new children into our other programs, their long term affiliation with the church often proves unsuccessful if the modeling of their parents contradicts what's being taught at church. The contacts with the children at Vacation Bible School should lead us to a personal ministry to the entire family. Cordial persistence with parents will let them know that we are sincere in our desire to have our church be a spiritual resource for their entire family.

Some churches in our area have switched to an

evening Bible school. What are the advantages and disadvantages to this VBS approach?

Numerically speaking, evening schools may not pull as many neighborhood children as a traditional daytime school. If you are seeking a large group of non-church, neighborhood kids to participate in the VBS, the daytime school will attract more students.

There are many advantages of an evening school, however, that may make this form of training worth trying. There are two major advantages.

First, people who work on day shifts are available to teach in the evening schools. For example, having men teach models that Christ is also for boys, helps maintain discipline, and shows a healthy relationship between a caring couple. Many of the VBS students may come from broken homes and will benefit from a couple working in harmony as well as the opposite sex role model.

Secondly, an evening Vacation Bible School can also offer adult classes. Neighborhood children are not our only mission field. The whole family is our concern. Adult electives on money management, divorce recovery, God's helps for human hurts, and so on, along with the use of good Christian films, can speak to any of the needs faced by the families in our communities.

What is meant by day clubs?

In addition to a Vacation Bible School, or as an alternative to it, some churches run summer day clubs. For example, a club might meet one day a week from 9 till noon for ten weeks. Juniors or junior highers might meet from 9 a.m. to 3 p.m. The clubs would utilize the normal activities of a Vacation Bible

School and extended clubs would use the afternoons for recreation.

Curriculum for day clubs would usually be a publishing house's Vacation Bible School materials. For instance, a ten day manual used one lesson per week. This approach maintains continuity with children throughout the summer, allows the whole summer for follow-up, and usually does not exhaust workers as in a five or ten-day program. In addition, a Bible study, craft, outreach, or mother's-day-out could also be scheduled for women during the same hours of the day clubs. Here, again, the teaching emphasis of the church would extend beyond the child to also include the parents.

What is the place of retreats and camps in the church program?

Retreats and camps have a very significant place in church ministry. They can be designed to meet all the purposes of the church: worship, education, fellowship and even evangelism. When a child is removed from the distractions of his own local environment, he is able to think more seriously about spiritual things. Because of the intensity and time involved in a weekend retreat or week long camp, the student can learn through the modeling of other students as well as the leaders. Many decisions for Christ, and recommitments to the Lord have taken place at retreats and camps.

The cost of camp varies. A week of camping may be difficult financially for families with many children. Since the experience is enriching to the child and supportive of the in-house programs of the church, the church should encourage and assist as many as possible to share in this learning opportunity.

Should our church encourage or sponsor neighborhood Bible clubs?

A church's support of special neighborhood ministries such as Good News Clubs largely depends on the church's own program and the quality of neighborhood ministry that can be offered.

Neighborhood clubs usually do not cost the church very much in resources. In some programs, facility, staff and program are not directly the responsibility of the church. Where the programs are of good quality, church encouragement through promotion to its members and some financial assistance are well worth the value of the club.

Usually the neighborhood Bible clubs are supplemental to the church's ministry and also serve as an evangelistic outreach. Since they take the message of Christ to some who would never come into the church facilities, encouraging support of these neighborhood ministries is worthy of consideration.

Several have suggested we begin a puppet ministry. What will this involve?

Puppets are vehicles of communication. Puppets can teach Bible truths; they can lead in music, and they can also offer children and young people an opportunity to minister to others in the body of Christ. They can be used by a youth group to minister in nursing homes, orphanages, prisons and children's centers. Puppets can be humorous and also serious. They can be a whole program, or part of a program, where the preaching theme is illustrated and introduced through the puppet dialogue.

The cost of a puppet ministry can vary greatly. One church

may choose to buy professional puppets, lighting, scripts and dialogues, whereas another church may choose to make their own puppets and equipment. A bibliography listing sources for quality puppets and a variety of scripts, is included at the end of this chapter. For those who choose to make their own puppets, a local library usually has pattern books which can be easily followed. A number of years ago *Family Circle* magazine also gave patterns for three different sized muppets.

An attractive stage can be made by using two-inch plastic piping for the frame and homemade curtains for the coverings. The pipes are light, fit snugly into each other, and the curtain tops have Velcro for attaching them over the bars. Set-up, take-down and storage is simple with this type of equipment.

Children and adults alike are fascinated by the ministry of puppets. Puppets can communicate feelings, techniques of witnessing, how to pray, Bible characters, and desirable attitudes and behaviors. One church even presented its entire new budget by the use of puppets. Are puppets effective? In the church that used puppets to present their new fiscal year, it was the first year the new budget was adopted unanimously!

How can we get and keep youth involved in our program?

It may seem trite to say, "People scratch where they itch," but any ministry that is going to draw and involve people must be one that is personally meaningful to them. The principles of growth and quality programming do not change when we are working with adolescents. There are uniquenesses to each age group, but the same principles remain.

Youth ministry is difficult for many because they fail to realize that teenagers are both children and adults. As children, the adults who work with them need to give them both high support and loving control. We cannot expect the young people to run their own programs, but neither should we try to run the programs for them. Responsibility must be shared in a cooperative way between the youth sponsors and key teenagers in the youth group.

The forms of youth programs vary. Some churches build their youth ministry around an outreach night which includes games and special music. Some groups utilize creative programming and after-church fellowships. For others, the Sunday School is the primary time for instruction and fellowship, with other activities serving to supplement the Sunday morning hour. Other youth groups thrive on puppet ministries, sports, or service projects which pull their young people together into a united group.

Since young people differ, we must be careful not to center the entire youth ministry around a particular emphasis. The youth choir, outreach team or puppet ministry can be a good vehicle, yet it can also become divisive. In the same way, a youth ministry that relies on sports can also scare off kids who are not athletic by nature. Sunday School, after-church activities, and a good balance of special events should be used to provide a diversified program to interest most young people.

The bottom line in any ministry is: (1) Does it interest me? (2) Do I feel welcomed and accepted at the activities? (3) Does someone show personal interest in me? and (4) Do I feel comfortable in inviting my friends to this program? The young people themselves are important in meeting these needs. A sensitive, energetic youth leader is also crucial in producing the above type of program. There are many materials written for youth ministry and a number of good youth seminars available. Carefully selected, trained leadership will produce a program guaranteed to keep teens involved.

God has provided everything each local congregation needs to effectively minister to its own people. Even the church at

Corinth, with all of its problems, had all the spiritual gifts. There are couples and singles who can work in youth ministries in each of our churches. Our responsibility is to recruit and encourage them, and then train and continually support them in their ministries to our teens. They will be the difference between a mediocre youth group and a dynamic youth ministry.

Our church is small and our youth group is small. How can we minister to our young people?

It is true. The dynamics of any group change with the size. For example, a dominant person or a troublemaker creates larger waves in a smaller group.

There are some disadvantages to a smaller youth group, but there are also many advantages. In a smaller group young people can develop a close camaraderie as they travel together in a van, minister in a nursing home, attend an inter-denominational youth rally, or have Saturday morning devotions in a neighborhood park.

Youth leaders who work in the Sunday School, mid-week service, or youth activities can have a long-lasting impact on the lives of teens. I still receive correspondence, two decades later, from a fellow who was in my junior high group when I sponsored that small fellowship as a college student. A quality program can be provided to kids, no matter what size fellowship.

Especially where the youth group is small, the leadership should implement creative and special activities. A Friday night movie once a month with other churches, an all-city church skating night, an ongoing, round-robin volleyball tournament, or a week at youth camp will allow young people to mix with other guys and gals on a larger group basis.

Flexibility in programming is easier, also, in the smaller youth group. An evening in the pastor's home for banana splits is more feasible with a smaller group, whereas that type of activity in a large church would take considerably more energy. God entrusted a certain number of kids to each youth group. Our faithfulness to those kids and their friends will lead to additional teens in our ministries.

Are church libraries cost effective with regard to their usage?

Church libraries are an excellent vehicle for supplementing the teaching ministry of a local church. Books, records, tapes and other materials available in the library can be used for enrichment, research for Bible studies, and even outreach to others. Libraries are a very significant tool for ministry, but the question remains, are they cost effective?

For a library to be cost effective it must have a high enough usage to justify the funds committed to this ministry. A library that is used often can justify a significant amount of money in a Christian education budget.

A balance should be sought between reference materials and contemporary Christian reading. A balance between tapes, records and books must also be sought. Donated books will cut expenses, but books should only be accepted and processed which will have a good circulation. While reference books are important, a few sets of good works are better than many different books. The reference section is essential, but is not used as much as the contemporary section.

Book reviews in Christian periodicals can make the library committee aware of classics and best sellers. Good quality, high interest books, tapes and records will make the library appealing. A library in constant use can then justify the needed funds for supplemental educational resources.

How can we encourage more people to use our church library?

There are three important ingredients to a growing library ministry: location, promotion and quality. If any of these concerns are overlooked, the effectiveness of the library will decrease. Usage of the library is directly related to all three ingredients.

The church library should be located in the most traveled area of the church campus. Usually this will mean it should be placed near the sanctuary, perhaps off the foyer. If there is a heavy traffic flow from a parking lot to the sanctuary, a room in the building between those locations might also prove beneficial. No one will use a library that is out of the way. If the library usage is to grow, its location must be obvious to people who are moving about the campus.

Ongoing promotion of the church library also helps to keep that ministry fresh in people's minds. They may travel past the library door every single Sunday, but not actually choose to go in until they read the title of a newly processed book in the church bulletin. Posters, notes in the church bulletin, announcements in the church newsletter, an occasional mailing, and reference to the library by the pastor or Christian education workers will all encourage people to use the material in the library.

Encouragement and announcements may bring people to the library, but if it is disorganized, unattractive, out-of-date or unappealing, it will be difficult to get the dissatisfied user to return. A good library must be attractive, well-stocked and of good quality. When the library is open, someone should be there who can answer questions regarding books or tapes. The personal touch of the librarian provides the finishing touch for a well-equipped, well-promoted and sensibly located library.

Is there anything wrong with developing our own programs?

During one school holiday our family visited Washington, D.C. Ben and Betsy agreed that their favorite part of the trip was visiting the Smithsonian Air and Space Museum. While the early aircraft were interesting, it was the space rockets that thrilled them most. The huge rockets and the Mercury, Gemini and Apollo capsules were a testimony of the ability of scientists to develop vehicles for travel to specific, exciting destinations. The Apollo missions were specifically designed to reach and study the moon. The special capsule, lunar lander, space suits, moon buggy and other equipment were all created to accomplish a predetermined task.

Similarly, the church exists to provide a vehicle for corporate worship, Biblical instruction, intimate fellowship, and evangelical witness. The function of doctrinal teaching will never change, but the forms we use to instill Christian truth will vary. The message is permanent; but our methods vary to give the message the maximum impact on a given group, at a given time.

There is nothing inherently wrong with a church developing its own programs. Who knows the needs of a local congregation better than the congregation itself? Before we take off building new vehicles, however, two questions should be raised: (1) What am I trying to accomplish that requires this new vehicle; and (2) Has someone else already invented a suitable vehicle?

Our Lord has told us to use our time wisely. There are only limited reasons for writing our own Sunday School materials or creating a new club program. There are many varieties already available that can be used directly or adapted for our needs.

On the other hand, there may be some specific educational emphasis that we desire which would best be served by our own created programs. For example, one church wanted their children to have a release time program on Sunday evenings, so they developed the 4-M Program. For thirty minutes each Sunday evening, while the pastor was preaching, they had a rotation program consisting of *m*usic, *m*issions, *m*ovies and *m*inistry. Four couples took one responsibility each, serving one Sunday every month. The ministry night was especially enjoyable for the children for they were able to make things (like fruitbaskets) which they shared with shut-ins, and participated in a variety of activities.

In another situation, a church developed a R.I.F. Program for children. This program also took place during the evening service, and helped third and fourth graders learn through the library. Through the *R*eading *I*s *F*un Program, the kids heard a story each Sunday evening and were challenged to check out books for weekday enjoyment.

Programs are vehicles for accomplishing purposes. We do not simply want to do what the church down the street does, neither do we want to reinvent the wheel. When we have defined and understand our church's educational goals, we may enjoy developing creative ways of reaching those goals.

Summary

When we watch a football game we see a collage of sets and plays. We observe running plays, passing attempts and kicking downs. After viewing several contests, we get an understanding of what football is all about.

When we study Christian education, we realize that our program is larger than just the Sunday School. There are many parts to an educational ministry, and when these emphases are played well together, successful learning occurs. Our goals of presenting all people mature in Christ will never change. The designing of a program to accomplish this goal will always be our exciting task.

PUPPETRY BIBLIOGRAPHY

Autry, Edward A. and Lola M. *Bible Puppet Plays.* Grand Rapids: Baker Book House, 1972.

Chapman, Marie. *Puppet Animals Tell Bible Stories.* Denver: Accent Books, 1977.

Chesse, Bruce and Armstrong, Beverly. *Puppets From Poly-Foam: Spongee-Es.* Walnut Creek, CA: Early Stages, 1975.

Goodrich, Meredith. *Finger Puppets Help Teach.* Denver: Accent Books, 1976.

Harp, Grace. *Handbook of Christian Puppetry.* Denver: Accent Books, 1984.

Magnet, Charles. *Puppet Dialogues.* Denver: Accent Books, 1978.

Marsh, Fredda with Mooney, Dow. *Putting It All Together In A Puppet Ministry.* Springfield: Gospel Publishing House, 1978.

Reynolds, Joyce. *Puppet Shows That Reach and Teach Children.* Springfield: Gospel Publishing House, 1972.

Robertson, Everett. *Using Puppetry In The Church.* Nashville: Convention Press, 1976.

Rodrick, Bruce. *Teaching With Puppets.* Cincinnati: Standard Publishing, 1975.

Rottman, Fran. *Easy To Make Puppets and How To Use Them.* Glendale: G/L Publications, 1978.

Warner, Diane. *Bible Puppet Scripts For Busy Teachers.* Denver: Accent Books, 1983.

Warner, Diane. *Puppets Help Teach.* Denver: Accent Books, 1975.

PROFESSIONAL PUPPETS, PATTERNS AND ACCESSORIES

Backes Patterns. P.O. Box 582, South St. Paul, MN 55075.

Professional Puppets of Florida. 5339 Lenox Ave., Jacksonville, FL 32205.

Puppet Masters. P.O. Box 11162, Palo Alto, CA 94306.

Puppet Pals Company. 100 Belhaven Drive, Los Gatos, CA 95030.

Puppet Productions. P.O. Box 82008, San Diego, CA 92138.

The Puppetry Store. P.O. Box 3128, Santa Ana, CA 92703.

4

DEVELOPING THE PLAY BOOK:
Curriculum

The field of athletics has players, organization, games, and written strategies to be executed in those games. When rookies enter training camp, one of their first jobs is to learn the play book. The strategies in it have been developed over several years by the coaches and tell the team what to do during a game. Good teams have good play books. They must be both basic, yet comprehensive. The success of the team depends on how well they follow the directions of each play.

In Christian education our games or programs are best played when good, basic curriculum, comprehensive for our needs, is followed by the players. Teachers who implement the lesson plans given in the curriculum, will be successful in helping their students learn more of God.

The questions in this chapter will focus our thoughts on curricula used in Christian education.

How can I learn what types of Christian education materials are available?

There are three good sources for finding out about C.E. materials. One good resource may be the local Christian bookstore. Some communities have excellent bookstores, whereas other stores may be ill-supplied in this area. The economy also affects bookstores, so the amount of materials they keep in stock varies from time to time.

However, bookstores usually have a sampling of Sunday School materials from several publishing houses. In addition, many have racks which display Bible study materials such as those of the Navigators, Campus Crusade for Christ, Moody Press, and Inter-Varsity Press. A Christian bookstore may be able to supply books and study aids for just about any C.E. program. Materials from denominational presses, or specific programs such as AWANA Clubs, however, are usually only available directly from those organizations.

Information on Christian education materials can also be found by keeping current with Christian periodicals. For example, *Moody Monthly* or *Eternity* magazines annually review books and study aids that can be useful in the church. Publishing houses also purchase advertising space in periodicals to promote everything from video cassettes to next summer's Vacation Bible School materials. Staying current with several Christian periodicals will help church leaders be aware of the latest in curricula.

A third source of information on Christian education materials is from leaders in other churches. Whether it be at a ministers' fellowship, or by program leaders in contact with leaders in other churches, regular interaction with others keeps us aware of new ideas and available materials. Getting together with leaders in sister churches not only promotes creativity and fellowship, but it is also beneficial in the building of ideas and resources.

Who in the church should be responsible for curriculum selection?

The Christian Education Committee in coordination with the leaders of a program should be responsible for curriculum selection. Individual teachers or workers within a program should be consulted and exposed to curriculum possibilities, but the decision should be made by the C.E. Committee or the leaders of a program.

Coordination of curricula is important, yet many churches fail to give adequate supervision to the coordination and sequencing of their curriculum. Students need a balance of Old Testament and New Testament; a blend of the biographical, historical and didactical; and a variety between book studies and topical studies. Allowing individual departments or teachers to select their own curriculum is not usually best for coordination.

The organization and size of your Sunday School is another factor in selection. A flexible curriculum can be implemented many ways.

The use of one publishing house for the whole curriculum in a given program will give the needed balance. For example, in the Sunday School the same publisher should be used for all ages. This practice will avoid the duplication of Bible passages that could happen from one grade to the next if different companies are used.

Most publishers produce a scope and sequence chart that describes the subject matter covered each quarter for every age. For example, one publishing house may cycle through the Bible in a conceptual form during the pre-school years, cycle through the Scriptures again from a story perspective in grades one through three, and then cycle through the Bible a third time from a historical perspective in grades four through six. A complete plan would also be presented for the six years of the youth division, with a variety of book studies and topical studies offered for adults.

To insure both balance and Bible coverage, one publishing house should be used for each program. A thorough study should be made as to which curriculum is best for a program, and then only essential changes in curriculum should be considered. The change should still follow the approved scope and sequence for the overall program.

How can we coordinate the teaching content presented in our various programs (i.e. Sunday School) with club ministry?

The best way to coordinate the teaching content of the various programs is to first establish the curriculum of the predominant program, or the program which is most attended, and then supplement those themes in the other educational programs. This is another reason for consistently using the scope and sequence of one publisher.

Since Sunday School is usually the church's largest educational program, other programs should supplement, not duplicate, what is being taught in the Sunday School. When the scope and sequence of the Sunday School is available to program leaders, they can develop their own plans without repetition. If they desire to teach the same Bible content, they can at least make the Sunday School staff aware of their objectives.

Here are two illustrations that occur frequently. When a youth sponsor seeks input on what to teach on Wednesday evenings or on the winter retreat, he can be given suggestions based on what is not being taught that year in the Sunday School.

Another example might be a women's Bible study that consults the pastor for topics or materials for its group. Knowing what the adult Sunday School will be teaching during the next two years, the pastor can make suggestions that will steer the group into different or complementary areas of study.

A balanced curriculum over several years can be planned ahead of time, when thought is first given to the content of the major program, and then supplemental studies planned for other programs.

Should teachers be allowed to develop their own materials, or is it best to use published curriculum?

Very few teachers are capable of producing their own materials. Many can explain a Bible passage, but few are able to plan a balanced sequence of curriculum, and then take that sequence and develop methodology which makes it beneficial to their particular age student.

Published materials provide a balance of themes, a variety of illustrative material, and presentations geared to the learner's conceptual level.

Occasionally a teacher will not like a particular lesson or learning activity suggested in the curriculum. In these cases, the teacher ought to have the freedom to substitute an alternate method in a given lesson if he or she is confident this activity is superior. In general, however, those who work full-time in the development of curriculum are more aware of learning needs, and appropriate methods for individual ages.

If a special program is begun, for example, as a release feature of a Sunday evening service, the staff may wish to develop their own materials. Even in this situation, however, careful attention should be given to what is taught in the other programs in the church, so that there can be coordination for the students.

A creative Christian education ministry can have room for both a predetermined, balanced curriculum, and opportunities for the learners to make choices for study. A flexible curriculum can follow a planned scope and sequence, but allow for student choice within the teaching methodology of individual lessons. In order to assure comprehensive Bible coverage for all of the congregation, more freedom should be offered in the supplemental educational programs rather than in the primary endeavor. Flexibility of study is more easily accomplished in mid-week studies, retreats, youth meetings, club programs and home studies.

In the childhood years, learner preferences are best accomplished by providing choices of learning activities within a predetermined lesson. With teens and adults, selection of whole topics of study can become their responsibility.

If a church desires to respond to student selection during the Sunday School hour, the summer quarter is usually a good time to vary a format. A survey of students could reveal specific topics they are interested in studying, and if a change in curriculum is to be made, the summer may be the most flexible time to vary the format.

In general, student input and desire can be responded to without varying far from a planned curriculum. Special assignments, optional meetings and a few sessions usually deal with most questions. A balance between a planned scope and sequence, and yet sensitivity to learner needs and individual questions, can be accomplished in a balanced, planned curriculum.

What are the benefits and drawbacks of electives for adults or youth?

Adults and youth should have opportunities for choice within the curriculum. A choice of electives in the Sunday School, mid-week program or through home studies will let the learners know the church is conscious of their concerns, and make them aware that they are responsible for their own spiritual growth. A completely predetermined curriculum offers no individual freedom; a total elective system minimizes the ability to provide a comprehensive and balanced curriculum.

Electives should be used for adults and youth. The program in which the selection is offered, however, is a more difficult question. The answer will vary depending on the overall Christian education offerings in each local church. The place of electives will also vary depending on other emphases in the church, such as fellowship, outreach and follow-up.

The advantages and disadvantages of using electives during the Sunday School hour are discussed further in the chapter on "Keeping the Team Going."

What are the pros and cons of dated versus non-dated materials?

In selecting a Sunday School curriculum, there are many questions that should be asked to determine which one is best for your church. Bible coverage, specific themes, methodology, and attractiveness of art work are just a few. Some Christian magazines provide a comparison of several publishing houses, contrasting them according to a number of factors. The issue of dated versus non-dated material is just one question which must be considered.

Non-dated material has the advantage of being reusable, which in the long run makes it less costly. When rotating the material on a two-year cycle, for example, it is possible to use the same material two to four times before a major rewriting is undertaken. Since the same material is retaught two or three years later, a teacher that stays in the department becomes familiar with the lesson material, should save time in preparation, and have better ease with the implementation of the lesson. A word of caution, however. Materials will only be less costly if they are filed properly and completely.

Dated material has one advantage of being initially less expensive. Since some teachers do not turn in their materials completely, it may prove as inexpensive as non-dated material in the long run.

A second advantage of dated material is that each course is new. It might not be totally new, since a partial rewrite of the material is not unusual. Greater care must also be exercised to order the right amount of materials when using dated material. The task of filing material and taking inventories before ordering is not essential when all new materials are ordered each quarter.

Since dated materials are not reusable in their intended program, good materials could be saved for supplemental teaching, or they can be channeled to missionaries or others who are looking for Bible related curriculum.

What are some ways to keep curriculum costs down?

The greatest way to keep curriculum costs down is to use what you choose. For example, if take-home papers are being read and appreciated by children and parents, then the cost of these supplemental papers is justifiable. If careful investigation reveals that half of the papers are turned into airplanes on Sunday morning, and the other half are filed away at home without being read, material costs can be cut by not purchasing these papers.

The same principle follows with all materials. If adults are using their quarterlies or the paperback books that are designed for their course, then these should be made available for them. In the adult division you have the option of letting adults that desire so, buy their own books, whereas in the children's division, the church must provide them. Nevertheless, if investigation reveals that adults are not preparing at home in advance, then again it might be wiser to make student books available in the church library, where they can be checked out by those who have real interest.

Teacher manuals and teacher aids are a must for every age group. Costs should not be cut in the resources provided for teachers. The in-class materials used by a student are also very important; they are actually part of the teaching session.

Careful filing of non-dated curriculum will also trim expenses. Finding a volunteer who will coordinate the curriculum files will be a ministry that will save the church significant amounts of money in curriculum over time.

Some programs, such as a children's church or club programs, will also have materials that may be reusable. The program leaders should check the cycle of those materials, since they will not want to repeat lessons until their students are promoted to another age group. These materials should be filed in a Christian education office, or in a central location, so that with staff turnover, there is still an awareness of materials that have been used, and where they are available for reuse.

In enrichment programs, such as a release-time feature for elementary children during a Sunday evening service, a program leader may use his or her own materials when approved by the Christian Education Committee. The church should offer to cover the expense of those materials, but many times the leader will just consider those costs a gift to the church.

The bottom line is, again, use what you choose. If you are using wisely the materials that are selected, curriculum costs will be justified and meaningful.

Where in our program should we have an emphasis on Bible memorization?

Last week during a special service, one of our teachers conducted a children's program while parents were in the sanctuary. The worker used an old edition of Bible Baseball as a learning activity for third through sixth graders. To her surprise she found that many of the children could not answer the "single" questions, let alone attempt a double, triple or home run. The amount of Bible knowledge that our children have committed to memory is decreasing in many churches.

Over the last couple of decades there has been a movement away from rote and detailed instruction. The size of Bible passages studied each week has been reduced, with the emphasis on more learning activities to reinforce lesson objectives. While this trend enhances the learning of certain Bible truths, even the regular Sunday School attender does not develop a mastery of the Bible with only church school participation.

Many parents who are aware of their children's Biblical illiteracy, and perhaps equally as important, are upset with their local public school's permissiveness, have placed their children in a Christian school. Children who attend Christian schools will grow faster in their knowledge of the Scriptures. With this trend, however, there is a new problem for the local church. There is a growing disparity among its students. Some have a very primitive knowledge of the Scriptures, others are bored when basics are presented. The disparity is too great, and many have adopted special programs to help with this need.

A reemphasis on Bible memorization is needed in our Christian education ministry. Every Bible lesson has a theme, and therefore should have a key verse underlying that theme. The teacher can stress this verse and expect a child to retain it over time. Ongoing review and carefully selected reward systems can make memorization very possible.

While memorization can be a part of every program, opportunity should also be provided for more extensive memorization. Elementary age children are memorizing large amounts of material for school including musical lyrics, plays and various other lessons. Since the students are capable of memorization, we should encourage them to hide God's Word in their hearts, too.

Some churches have moved to utilizing the club program as the primary vehicle for memorization. One of the main component parts of the AWANA program, for example, is the memorization of Scripture. Wherever the memory emphasis is made, the learning of Scripture verses, their meaning and application, should be part of the educational ministry. The purpose is not to have a child simply memorize 300 verses. No. Our desire is that he understand the Scriptures; and that his memorization will program his conscience to behave in light of those verses.

Rote memorization apart from meaningful understanding has little significance. Worse yet, however, is no memorization at all. A balance of memorization, with a stress on meaning and application, should be part of a balanced educational program.

Should homework be assigned to students?

The purpose of homework is to stretch each teaching session.

It is given to help students make personal discoveries for themselves, and to practice things in greater depth for mastery. Just as homework is used in grade school, high school, college and other training seminars, homework can be beneficial also in our Christian education programs.

There are several difficulties with assigning homework in our Christian education programs, though. The first problem is that most people believe the church is to be a place where they attend passively and listen to a preacher or a Bible class teacher. After a hard week of work, many come to church for a worship experience, or to hear a Bible teacher explain the Scriptures. The concept of being actively involved in learning, involved even to the point of doing personal study or research, is foreign to the mindset of many. The church fosters this concept by providing only impressional programming.

The second difficulty with utilizing homework in the church school is that meetings are seven days apart. Accountability and follow-up are hard to enforce. However, as a teacher begins to assign homework occasionally, and then more regularly in his class, students will grow more accustomed to their responsibility as an active learner. The teacher, of course, must consistently follow up his responsibility by calling for the homework and giving positive reinforcement to those who do it.

In most Sunday Schools, homework is usually restricted to having a Bible verse memorized for the following Sunday. While good, this repetitive predictability stifles the natural creativity of children. Many are willing to take on assignments outside of the classroom. Many adults are also willing to bring back a report on a class question the following Sunday. It is certainly true that the class will benefit from the student's research and report, but the student will grow the most, finding that he can study apart from the tutelage of the teacher.

Valuable instructional time can be extended beyond the classroom by asking students to make a map of the city of

Jerusalem, interview friends on what they think God is like, or write a modern newspaper account of the exodus. Not only will learning be maximized through the extended time available for the homework, but the repetition of the study at home will deepen the student's understanding. In addition, individual involvement with the material will build personal study skills and enhance learning.

Should tests be used to measure learning?

Evaluation is something seldom practiced in the church. Most programs run year after year without critique; most teachers are never assessed; most curriculum is just ordered automatically; and even pastoral staff members are rarely allowed the benefit of evaluation.

Tests are designed to measure learning, but usually for the purpose of grading. Since ranking of students has no practical value in the church, regular detailed testing of subject matter will probably have little worth.

While detailed tests might prove threatening (especially to adults who have passed the years of school testing, and may also be embarrassed by their lack of Bible knowledge), periodic assessment can be used if handled carefully. Through questions and answers, observation of discussion groups, and informal probing, a teacher can glean an understanding of how the students are doing. Occasional surveys and questionnaires can be used for student self-evaluation, as well as informing the teacher of learner concerns.

For example, to know that three members of a class have mastered 80 percent of the content of the Gospel of John is not really that significant. But, to know that eight out of seventeen surveys indicated a felt inadequacy regarding defending Christian teachings would communicate quite a lot.

Tests can be used for measuring learning, but they can also be used as a teaching method. Questions at the end of a lesson in a student quarterly, or assigned as preparation for next week's passage, can be a valuable teaching technique which is relatively non-threatening.

How important is it for parents to be aware of their children's curriculum?

Unfortunately, if you were to ask parents what their children were studying this quarter in Sunday School, probably less than two percent would be aware of the main theme and/or Scripture portion, let alone what the child is expected to learn and apply. Some parents ask their children what they are currently studying in class, but the child's response is only as informative as is his nature to share. For example, parents who have boys are usually more frustrated trying to elicit information than parents who have talkative little girls. Since communication through children to parents is limited, teachers should make opportunities to regularly contact their students' parents.

The purpose of informing parents regarding the child's curriculum goes beyond mere information. The parents are accountable to God for the Christian training of their child. The church's Christian education program should really be a supplement to the discipleship of their children. If the church and home are to work as partners, parents must have adequate communication from their child's teacher.

Communication with parents is best established early and comprehensively. In the beginning of each new Sunday School quarter, or at the beginning of a change in program, an overview of the course should be shared. Scriptural passages, themes and behavioral applications should be spelled out early. In addition, periodic communication with the home and an open house two or three times a year, can be used to keep parents informed and relationships of high quality.

What is your assessment of the growing field of video cassettes?

The 1980s have seen an explosion in the use of video cassettes. Videos are now used by restaurants to entertain customers; by salesmen to introduce new products; and by a growing number of families for home entertainment. The rapid growth of video cassettes in the secular market is having a parallel proliferation in the church. Nationally known speakers, Sunday School experts, and even contemporary music artists have produced video cassettes. While we may not appreciate every title, even in the religious market, nevertheless this new medium is growing in impact on Christians.

And, the Christian education ministry of the local church can benefit through a balanced use of video cassettes. While a church does not *need* outside experts, there is value in a respected Bible teacher reinforcing the truths that are already being taught in a congregation.

One church used occasional video cassettes for their mid-week program during the summer. The messages on evangelism supplemented their class sessions. On another occasion the church had an all-day prayer seminar which used a combination of lectures by video, and an in-house discussion leader. In one congregation, four video cassettes which presented sample teaching sessions were rented. Four recorders and monitors were set up at the church, and the teachers in early childhood, children, youth and adults were able to watch and discuss a lesson given to their own age group.

The church in which I previously served used a six part series on "Brokenness" by Dr. Charles Stanley for their Wednesday evening service, and plan to use the series by R. C. Sproul on "The Holiness of God" to kick-off their upcoming fall mid-week program. Six videos every other year was an enjoyable change of pace, but not too much of a good thing.

Video cassettes can be used as a change in regular church programming, but they also have a place in home or retreat situations. A youth worker may bring a few videos to the senior high retreat. If plans need modification because of inclement weather, a video-recorded speker or music concert becomes a welcomed substitute. In one church the pastor purchased a video cassette of Dr. Joseph Aldrich speaking on "Building Redemptive Relationships." The video was initially shown to a small group at the church, and subsequently in several home Bible studies. One individual who worked evenings even checked the tape out of the library to study on his own.

The cost of video cassettes prohibits most churches from building a large video library. However, as more and more people purchase VCRs, a good media library will add a few titles whenever finances are available. We must guard against overuse and dependency on this new medium, but we should take advantage of the added diversity offered by this resource. A list of video cassette distributors is given at the end of this chapter.

Summary

Very few athletes make it to the height of professional sports. Only the most talented and disciplined are sought by a team. Most people will never know what it means to be a part of that kind of team.

What a contrast there is for the Christian, however! It is not the gifted, not the hard workers, not the privileged few who are selected to be on God's team. No matter what background or talents, the invitation of our Lord goes out to "whosoever will." When an individual confesses his sin and receives Jesus Christ as his personal Savior and Lord, he instantly becomes a member of the greatest team in the world. The plan of salvation is complete when all men are presented mature in Christ Jesus (Colossians 1:28).

In order to accomplish this purpose, Christian education programs are designed to instruct our people. God has given us one Training Manual, the Bible, which is the basis for developing the lessons that we use in our programs. Everyone in the body of Christ is a minister and player (I Corinthians 12; II Corinthians 5:14-21). God has given organization and leadership to His team.

Our play book (curriculum) is a compilation of Scriptural truths developed for the coaches so that they can train players, no matter what age or skill level. The play book is essential for a knowledgeable, organized team, and an effective play book is one which best communicates the Owner's Contractual Content, the Bible.

SAMPLE CHART FOR CURRICULUM FLEXIBILITY

			AGE	A	B	C
Closely Graded Courses	Preschool	Bible Beginnings	2	Courses for 2s	Rotate courses for 2s & 3s on a 2 year cycle	Use Kindergarten courses adapting for younger children
			3	Courses for 3s		
	Kindergarten		4	Courses for 4s	Rotate courses for 4s & 5s on a 2 year cycle	
			5	Courses for 5s		
			GRADE	A	B	C
	Primary Department	Bible Theology	1	Courses for 1st grade	Courses for 1st grade	Rotate courses for 1st, 2nd & 3rd grades on a 3 year cycle
			2	Courses for 2nd grade	Rotate courses for 2nd & 3rd grades on a 2 year cycle	
			3	Courses for 3rd grade		
	Junior Department	Bible Survey	4	Courses for 4th grade	Rotate courses for 4th & 5th grades on a 2 year cycle	Rotate courses for 4th, 5th & 6th grades on a 3 year cycle
			5	Courses for 5th grade		
			6	Courses for 6th grade	Courses for 6th grade	
Departmentally Graded	Junior High	Bible Establishing	7 8 9	Three Year Course—Junior Highs can meet in one class or in 3 separate classes—all will study the same course		
	High School	Bible Equipping	10 11 12	Three Year Course—High Schoolers can meet in one class or in 3 separate classes—all will study the same topics		
	Adults	Bible Exposition	Adult College Career	Ten Year Course—Different courses every quarter for 10 years, then cycle is repeated		

SUNDAY SCHOOL

From Accent on Life Bible Curriculum, Accent Publications, Denver

VIDEO CASSETTE RESOURCES

Some Christian bookstores are now selling video cassettes. A number of larger churches record special programs or key messages by their pastor. Most distributors of Christian films are increasing their library of rental videos.

Videos for purchase and/or rental are currently available from the following distributors:

American Video, P.O. Box 20330, Jackson, MS 39209.

Augsburg Publishing House, Box 1209, Minneapolis, MN 55440.

Conservative Baptist Audio Visuals, P.O. Box 66, Wheaton, IL 60189.

David C. Cook Publications, 850 North Grove Avenue, Elgin, IL 60120.

Gospel Films, P.O. Box 455, Muskegon, MI 49442.

Here's Life Publications, Inc., P.O. Box 1576, San Bernardino, CA 92402.

International Films, 235 Shaftebury Ave., London, WC2H BEL.

Knowledge Industry Publications, Inc., 701 Westchester Ave., White Plains, NY 10604. (Recently published a new directory entitled, "Home Video Marketplace.")

National Institute of Biblical Studies, 4001 North Dixon Hwy., #204, Pompano Beach, FL 33064.

New Day Productions, 3934 Sandshell, Forth Worth, TX.

Scripture Union Publishing, 1716 Spruce St., Philadelphia, PA 19103.

Tyndale House Publications, 336 Gundersen Drive, Wheaton, IL 60189.

Word Publications, 4800 West Waco Drive, Waco, TX 76796.

Worldwide Productions, 1201 Hennepin Avenue, Minneapolis, MN 55403.

5

MAKING THE TEAM A WINNER— Part One: Training

When I think of training, I think of C.C. Edwards. Coach Edwards drilled the basics into me when I was playing college tennis. At the beginning of each season the fellows were eager to get out and hit the ball. We wanted to play matches and challenge for position. The coach, however, had a predetermined sequence of drills that he supervised at the beginning of each season.

We would stroke forehand to forehand; backhand to backhand; and backhand to forehand. Each player would serve a bushel of balls daily toward two marked spots on the court. Footwork and position, net and volley, lob and smash were all methodically practiced.

Although we had only one really superior player on our ten man team, we placed high in the conference each season. The reason? Coach Edwards believed in training. He was committed to making us the best we could be with the talent that we had.

We have all heard the expression, "If something is worth doing, it is worth doing well." I cannot think of a task that is more worthwhile than teaching people about God and His expressed will. Two things are eternal: God's Word and people. The greatest task in which we can be involved is building God's Word into people. Effective teaching takes training.

Why is training important?

If we really believe that the Bible presents God's only way of salvation, and that the Bible contains God's clear principles for living, each teacher must do his or her very best to communicate those eternal and life-changing principles. Teacher training is the vehicle that helps teachers become more effective communicators of the Bible. It proves itself beneficial in three ways:

1. Teacher training is beneficial to the student. The better a teacher is able to communicate and motivate, the greater the understanding the students will have of God's Word.
2. Teacher training encourages the teacher. Teaching can be very frustrating, but teaching can also be a lot of fun. The individual who understands how to speak at the students' level, how to maintain classroom control, and how to use a variety of methods to communicate the Scriptures will usually enjoy his or her teaching experience. A teacher who applies what has been learned in training sessions will grow less discouraged, and will become more confident in the ability to teach.
3. Teacher training strengthens the congregation as a whole. The very existence of training opportunities lets the average congregant realize that we are all people in process. None of us is a finished product. Even an experienced teacher still has much to learn. A new recruit can be assured of help in the areas in which he feels deficient. Training opportunities

demonstrate to the congregation that we all need to improve our serving skills.

How do educational workers respond to training opportunities?

Where a church has never given much emphasis to training, the beginning of a systematic teacher training program will be met with mixed reactions. Some of your newer teachers, or perhaps those who are younger in the faith, will be glad to have someone give them help. A teacher who has been teaching for many years may be less open to suggestions or ways of changing what he or she has been doing.

A church should aim at having an ongoing training program. Once this has been established, time will make it as routine and expected as the Sunday morning sermon and offering.

In an earlier chapter we mentioned the importance of job descriptions and teaching contracts. It should be stated in writing that teachers are required to participate in departmental training, and that they will be encouraged to share in other opportunities. When the requirements are stated up front, teachers are more likely to fulfill their agreed upon commitment.

Should the program leaders require regular staff meetings?

Regular staff meetings are essential for several reasons.
1. They remind the teachers that they are not working alone, but are part of a team ministry of discipleship.
2. They provide an opportunity for the ministry team to pray together, jointly asking God to use their service and touch the lives of their students.

3. They give teachers a set time for planning, to insure that each person knows his responsibility for the coming lesson.
4. They offer the teachers opportunities to share their problems and receive suggestions from one another.

All of our people are very busy. How can I expect them to give time for training?

This question accurately portrays American life. It used to be primarily the medical doctor and the business executive who rushed through the day meeting deadlines. Today, though, even retired grandmothers have too many things to do on their daily schedule.

In our own mind, and in the minds of our teachers, we need to continually lift up our high calling. When we consider the temporal and the eternal, we realize that there is no greater task than sharing the eternal Word with people who have an eternal future. We must expect our staff to pursue training. If we do not have that expectation, many of them will not either.

We need to be careful, however, that we have good balance in our training approach. Major training opportunities, such as a Sunday School convention or a visiting workshop leader, should be planned well in advance. People should put these dates on their calendars, and frequent, enthusiastic reminders should be made to keep the dates fresh in their minds. Because of schedule pressures, large group training sessions should be kept to a minimum.

Ongoing, regular training, though, should be conducted within each program, division or department. These departmental meetings will necessitate coordinating the schedules of far fewer people.

A monthly or bimonthly meeting of departments is beneficial, and the dates for these meetings can be established ahead of time for the entire year. For example, the primary workers may meet on the first Tuesday of each month, while the Boys Brigade staff meet for an hour after their last monthly club night. Advanced, regular and consistent scheduling will stress the importance of our task and will help people make training a priority in their schedules.

What percentage of our staff can we expect to pursue training?

We should expect one hundred percent of our staff to pursue training! Some will be enthusiastic, some will be ambivalent, and some may resist or demonstrate occasional absenteeism. Nevertheless, we must expect all of our teachers to be open to the Lord's refining of their gifts and abilities.

If a teacher demonstrates a lack of interest in improving his skills, he should give serious consideration to whether or not he really wants to renew his annual teaching assignment when his term expires.

What can teachers do on their own to improve their teaching?

There are many things that teachers can do at their own time and pace, and within their own environment. Individually, a teacher could attend a Christian education conference or seminar. But three areas for self-improvement are available to all of our teachers.

1. *Reading.* Reading educational articles in Christian magazines or books on teaching can be very helpful. They motivate

the teacher, give practical suggestions for the classroom, and also let the teacher know that he is not alone in the learning process. Most publishing houses produce materials which focus on learner needs and the process of teaching. Correspondence courses, such as those of Moody Bible Institute, deal with a variety of subjects that enrich the teacher. Teacher training cassette tapes on a variety of subjects are also available for the person who prefers listening to reading.

2. *Observing.* Since we learn best through modeling, a teacher can receive personal benefit from observing the classroom behavior of a good teacher. At least once or twice a year the teacher may want to arrange for a substitute for his own class, so that he can go into another class. He may even visit a good teacher in another church. The program leader should coordinate and set up these opportunities. Pastors know which of their ministerial friends would be open to allowing visitors into their programs. Begin by encouraging your program leaders to make the initial observations. They could then compile a list of competent teachers and good running programs that would be suitable for observation by their teachers.

3. *Sharing.* Teachers can learn much from discussion with other workers on how they prepare and interact with their students. The teacher should also be very open with his or her pupils, asking them where they "itch" and how they learn best.

Is group training more profitable than an individual learning by himself?

Some people enjoy the fellowship of a group; some prefer to

spend their free moments alone. Some individuals like to do a job by themselves; others prefer the company of co-workers. In Christian education, both group training and individual learning are profitable, and people will benefit differently from each.

Here are some benefits of group training:

1. Group training produces a camaraderie among the group members. Individually we can learn the essential ingredients of a lesson plan, but as we study that procedure together, we have the by-product of a growing closeness.

2. Group training is necessary for those who teach together. A department or program staff will benefit by planning and training as a group since they will be functioning together weekly.

3. Group teaching is time-efficient for the trainer. Many teachers can benefit from a new suggestion on preparation; many share the same difficulty of trying to accomplish too much within their class hour. The leader or consultant can deal with common problems through group training.

4. Some individuals are very sensitive to criticism, even positive suggestions that are shared in love. Suggestions made to a group are often less threatening to this type of person.

5. Group training makes possible the cross-pollination of ideas. The weight of instruction does not rest on the leader alone, but is also shared by all those present.

6. Some people just do not have the motivation to study on their own. If they are to learn how to be a better teacher, they need the accountability of a group, or an external schedule, to help them be disciplined.

Christian education is very much an "attitude." We should, therefore, capitalize on every opportunity for team building.

How important is it that our teachers attend outside workshops, seminars or Sunday School conventions?

While the regular staff meetings provide an opportunity for planning the details of each specific program, the larger training experience provides motivation. Sunday School conventions and other seminars will provide the teacher with a lot of practical how-tos. In addition, and of equal importance, is the personal encouragement and motivation gained through this opportunity.

The department meeting lets the teacher know he's part of a team ministry. Community workshops broaden the teacher's perspective of his significance even further. He's more than a Berean class teacher, he's part of a comprehensive network of leaders who are teaching God's Word throughout their community, their state and their nation.

The speaker brought in to these workshops have usually proved themselves as good models. Therefore, in addition to what they say, they will likely be demonstrating attitudes, values, behaviors and methods that may rub off on the teacher. While the outside seminar leaders may say the same thing you have told your people, it is good for them to hear that identical challenge presented from another reputable source.

Should the church subsidize the expense for

training, or should the teacher pay his own expenses?

When I first began working as a Christian Education Director, our church could not afford to subsidize the training of teachers. I simply encouraged teachers to come with me to various training opportunities at their own expense. The cost of the Sunday School conventions was nominal, but the cost of seminars was prohibitive to some.

As our church grew larger, we were able to place into the Christian education budget several hundred dollars for teacher training. We moved to the other extreme of completely reimbursing people for their conference expenses. We felt that if a person was willing to take a day off from work, or give up a Saturday for training, he should not also have to pay for that willing commitment. Interestingly, however, when we paid the full fee, our "no show" rates at the seminars began to increase. After two years we began to realize that when people make a personal commitment of funds, they are more likely to fulfill their commitment.

I believe the best arrangement is to solicit from your workers a non-refundable registration fee for the conference. The church should then pay any additional cost for the teacher to attend the seminar. In a seminar that costs $40, for example, the sponsoring organization may charge a $10 registration fee. The church could allow the teacher to pay the $10 fee (or perhaps even charge them $20) with the balance paid by the church. Because the teacher has made a personal investment, he or she will be more likely to attend the seminar. If the person does not show up for the seminar, most organizations refund all but the registration fee. In this way the individual is out his or her registration fee, but the church is protected from losing its money.

Should we have an outside expert come in to train our people?

The outside expert coming in to your congregation provides the same type of motivation received from attending a large Sunday School convention or training workshop. Depending on the proximity of available resource persons, a few evening presentations throughout the year can be very beneficial.

You could have a general session with the speaker from 7 p.m. to 7:50 p.m., a twenty minute coffee break, and then two or three elective training sessions from 8:10 p.m. to 9 p.m. The resource person could then be used to lead one of the electives in an area of specific need. A Saturday seminar might include two sessions in the morning, small-group or departmental meetings after lunch and a concluding, general session from 2:15 p.m. to 3 p.m.

It is difficult to charge people for in-house training. In order to get the most for your money, then, you should get the most qualified person you can from a relatively close geographical location. If money is no object, go for the best you can. But since finances are usually a real consideration, use your money for a worthy honorarium by keeping travel expenses to a minimum.

What things should be part of a teacher's training? What should he or she know to be a good teacher?

In each class session the teacher has an objective toward which he points his students. More generally, however, the teacher's *person* is more significant that the teacher's *presentation*.

Paul told the Colossians that he labored and worked with all the energy that God supplied so that he could present people mature in Christ. With continued exposure, students will pick up many of the attitudes, values, and even mannerisms of a respected teacher. Therefore, anything that helps a teacher become more like Jesus Christ is a valid ingredient for teacher training.

However, for effective teacher preparation and presentation, training should be provided in the following areas:

- A study of how learning takes place.
- Characteristics of the learner.
- Spiritual disciplines for the teacher.
- Understanding and utilizing teacher materials.
- An overview of teaching methods.
- The importance of application.
- Evaluating the teaching.

The most practical training for a teacher will be implementing training that relates directly to his or her program. Sunday School teachers will benefit from the planning session suggestions in their teacher's manuals. Children's club workers can study club training manuals to understand how each session should best function.

General works on training can be used to help teachers understand all parts of their jobs from preparation to presentation. A list of resources for teacher training is provided at the end of the chapter.

How can I help my teachers become more confident?

Confidence grows when we know that we're doing the right job well. Success breeds success. As leaders we need to encourage our teachers, letting them know that we believe in them. We need to affirm their involvement in the most important task in the world. In spite of human shortcomings and idiosyncrasies, we need to let each teacher know that he is an important part of the great work of Jesus Christ in building His church.

A teacher's confidence is also related to several other factors. These are the areas in which he or she must assume responsibility.

1. Understanding the learners. The greater the teacher's knowledge of the characteristics and needs of his students, the more responsive the class will be to his instruction. Their responsiveness, in turn, builds the teacher's confidence.

2. Knowing the subject matter. The teacher must be personally convinced that he has made a thorough study of the lesson. Even though he may be sharing a Scripture portion where there are different interpretations, he must be knowledgeable of the text and ready to share his convictions based upon it.

3. Working with the teaching-learning process. We can never assume that just because someone is moving his mouth, another individual is learning. A teacher's confidence grows as he knows how to involve the student, and help him make a personal application of the material.

4. Evaluating the teaching. When the astronauts traveled to the moon, there were times when they had to make necessary directional corrections. Evaluation is essential to determine if we are on target. By stating where we should be going, and then assessing whether or not we are on track, we will do the best job. Whether a teacher uses self-evaluation forms, listens to a cassette of his own teaching session, or has an outside observer sit in his classroom, he can grow in confidence through evaluation.

5. Believing in the sovereignty of God. When the teacher develops a Messiah complex, that he or she alone is the only link with an individual's spiritual health, undue pressure results. A teacher grows in confidence when he is simply faithful in presenting the Scriptures in an understandable way to the learner. He must leave the results to God.

Can you make a suggestion on a comprehensive training program for all of our educational workers?

While it is essential that each Christian education program has training which is specifically designed for it, there is also a great benefit in having an overall training program. Whether a person assists in children's church, teaches in the Sunday School, or works as a youth advisor, each one should be able to participate in the training program, and expectations must be realistic.

A number of years ago *Moody Monthly* magazine carried an article on a teacher training program called LEROY. While serving at the College Church in Wheaton, Illinois, Dr. Roy Zuck developed this creative approach. LEROY is an acronym for the comprehensive, five part training program. LEROY stands for:

L—*Leadership Training.* To meet this requirement the worker must complete a twelve hour Christian education course. The course could be conducted in the church, taken at a seminar or worked out independently by correspondence.

E—*Evaluation.* To receive credit for this part of the program, the teacher has another person evaluate one of his or her class sessions. The evaluator uses a standard form, shares the data with the teacher, and then leaves the form with the teacher.

R—*Reading.* To meet this qualification the Christian education worker must read at least 300 pages related to his or her area of teaching from an approved list.

O—*Observation.* This requirement is met when the worker observes another individual's class. Again, the coordinator of this program would make the necessary assignment, and an observation form should be used.

Y—*Yearly Conference.* This criteria is met when the worker attends a yearly Sunday School convention, participating in one general session and two workshops. One church allowed the substitution of three cassette messages from an approved list.

To keep motivation high, LEROY workers were recognized in the morning service. They were presented with a special certificate of achievement, and their pictures were displayed together. Once a LEROY worker was certified, we only required that he pursue three of five areas annually for recertification.

Sample forms and documents related to the LEROY program are provided at the end of this chapter.

Summary

When I visited my friend who coaches the Vermont Reds, each afternoon we would leave for the ballfield three hours before the game. Jack would pitch batting practice. Other coaches and team leaders would supervise the outfielders, infield practice, and pitching.

These young men were better than average ball players. They would not have made it as professionals without the necessary ability. If the Reds were to go on to win the double A title, however, they had to develop their skills to peak performance.

Two months later the Reds did win their World Series. How? Their dedication to training.

If something is worth doing, it *is* worth doing well! Is it worthwhile to teach people the Scriptures? Most certainly! The time, energy and finances necessary to do a superior job of training the Lord's teachers are resources well spent.

RESOURCES FOR TRAINING TEACHERS

Beechick, Ruth. *Training Preschoolers: It's Not Exactly Easy, But Here Is How To Do It.* Denver: Accent Books, 1979.

Beechick, Ruth. *Teaching Kindergartners: How To Understand and Instruct Fours and Fives.* Denver: Accent Books, 1980.

Beechick, Ruth. *Teaching Primaries: Understanding How They Think and How They Learn.* Denver: Accent Books, 1980.

Beechick, Ruth. *Teaching Juniors: Both Heart and Head.* Denver: Accent Books, 1981.

Creative Leadership For Christian Growth. (Three One-Year Media Kits) Elgin, IL: David C. Cook, 1984.

Dyet, James T. *Getting Through To Adults: Survival and Success In The Adult Classroom.* Denver: Accent Books, 1980.

125

Ford, Leroy. *A Primer For Teachers and Leaders.* Nashville: Broadman Press, 1963.

Gangel, Kenneth O. *Understanding Teaching.* Wheaton, IL: ETTA, 1968.

Martin, Dorothy. *Understanding and Guiding The Student.* Chicago: Moody Bible Institute Correspondence School, 1969.

Reed, Ed and Reed, Bobbie. *Creative Bible Learning For Youth.* Glendale, CA: International Center for Learning, 1977.

Richards, Lawrence O. *You The Teacher.* Chicago: Moody Press, 1972.

Richards, Lawrence O. *Creative Bible Teaching.* Chicago: Moody Press, 1970.

Senter III, Mark. *The Art of Recruiting Volunteers.* Wheaton: Victor Books, 1983.

Teaching With Results. Chicago: Moody Bible Institute Correspondence School, 1972.

Towns, Elmer L. *How To Grow An Effective Sunday School.* Denver: Accent Books, 1979.

Understanding People. Wheaton: Evangelical Teacher Training Association, 1972.

Understanding Sunday School. Wheaton: Evangelical Teacher Training Association, 1981.

Westing, Harold J. *Make Your Sunday School Grow Through Evaluation.* Wheaton: Victor Books, 1976.

Westing, Harold J. *The Super Superintendent.* Denver: Accent Books, 1980.

INSIDE OF LEROY BROCHURE

Questions and Answers:

1. *"What is LEROY?"*
   Ans. It is a five part voluntary certification program for our Christian Education Workers.

2. *"What does LEROY mean?"*
   Ans. The word is an acrostic and thus has five points or parts.
   L—*Leadership Course.* Complete at least one Christian Education course from one of the local Bible Colleges, our own Christian Life Institute, or take a correspondence course.
   E—*Evaluation.* Have a qualified person, approved by the C.E. Committee evaluate one of your class or group sessions.
   R—*Reading.* Read at least 300 pages from an approved reading list compiled by the C.E. Committee.
   O—*Observation.* Observe a class or group in another church comparable to the one in which you serve.
   Y—*Yearly Conference.* Attend at least one general session and two workshops at a Sunday School convention or similar training conference.

3. *"How can LEROY help me?"*
   Ans.
   *It is flexible and fully self-programmed. You can proceed at the pace best suited to you.
   *It will broaden your training beyond "just another training course."

*It has built-in options to meet your individual needs and interests.
*It is easy for you to achieve and yet difficult enough to present a significant challenge.

4. *"Why should I volunteer to earn the LEROY award?"*
   Ans. It will help you to remain current by learning new methods for making the application of the Bible relevant to today's students.

   As you and others gain certification, the quality of instruction in the Christian Education program will improve. Each doing a better job for the Lord's glory.

5. *"OK, how do I work toward certification?"*
   Ans.
   a. Take the "Record of Progress" and decide which point of LEROY you want to complete first, second, and so on.
   b. Write your name and date on the "Record of Progress" by each point when you complete it.
   c. Have your department head sign your "Record of Progress" when you have completed all five points. Then give it to the Minister of Education.
   d. Next, a properly signed and framed certificate will be publicly presented to you in the evening service.
   e. Each year thereafter—complete three of the five points to renew your certification.

RECORD OF PROGRESS

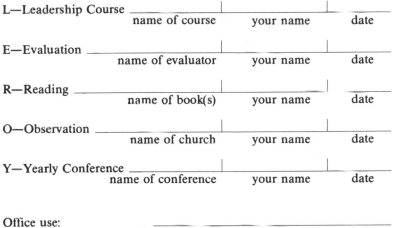

L—Leadership Course _____|_____|_____
               name of course   your name   date

E—Evaluation _____|_____|_____
        name of evaluator   your name   date

R—Reading _____|_____|_____
       name of book(s)   your name   date

O—Observation _____|_____|_____
       name of church   your name   date

Y—Yearly Conference _____|_____|_____
       name of conference   your name   date

Office use:
Certification issued   Signature of Department Head

LEROY RECORD CARD

This card is kept by the coordinator of training. One card is kept on file for each teacher. Progress of the entire staff can be kept up-to-date in a central file.

NAME: (last, first)

L—_____ _____
     name of course date

E—_____ _____
     name of evaluator date

R—_____ _____
     name of book(s) date

O—_____ _____
     name of church date

Y—_____ _____
     name of conference date

Certification Issued

_____

In Recognition

of training completed in the
Certification program
and of dedication in the Lord's work

_____ Church
Christian Education Committee
hereby grants to

CERTIFICATION

for the twelve-month period beginning _____

Certified Christian Education Worker

_____
PASTOR

_____
MINISTER OF CHRISTIAN EDUCATION

_____
CHAIRMAN OF CHRISTIAN EDUCATION
COMMITTEE

THE LEROY AWARD

6

MAKING THE TEAM A WINNER— Part Two: Methods

A pitcher's job is to keep the opponent's batters from scoring. Ideally, he will throw a variety of pitches with such accuracy that he will keep the batters from reaching base. He will try to deceive them with a curve ball, blow a fast ball by them, or throw a low slider with the hope that, at best, they will hit the ball on the ground for a forced out. The success of his team will depend, in part, on how well he uses the variety of pitches available to him.

Similarly, the Christian teacher plays well when he or she uses a variety of pedagogical strategies. The educator's task is to instill specific Biblical truths so that students can make personal application and grow in wisdom and knowledge of the Lord. In order to accomplish this task the teacher may pitch a discussion question, use a role play, or assign a research project. There are scores of methods available to Christian education workers. Success in the lives of students will depend in part on how well teachers use the variety of methods available to them.

Why do teachers' manuals suggest so many different methods? Can't students just study the Bible?

People are different from each other. Some prefer to read the account of an event, while others like to see the movie. Some people are very musical, but others "can't carry a tune in a bucket." Some like to work with their hands, while others would rather buy something ready made.

Using a mixture of teaching methods is not a trick for spicing up a Sunday School lesson. It is recognizing that students differ in the way they learn and trying to accommodate those differences. The goal of Christian education is to teach all things that Christ has commanded (Matthew 28:20). Therefore, it is important to maximize each student's ability to learn.

Offering a variety of instructional methods also encourages learning mastery. At the beginning of class a teacher may tell a Bible story with the help of visuals, followed by an activity page. Two or three Bible games could be used to reinforce the lesson. A short test might follow to measure the students' understanding, and, as it is self-corrected, serve as another teaching vehicle. The words of a song review the lesson theme, and drawing a poster again reinforces the message. The teacher's final summary, perhaps on a flip-chart, along with a review of the memory verse will give a final impact to the lesson.

A variety of teaching methods reinforces the Bible lesson several ways during the hour. The changes of pace also work with the students' attention spans. Mastery in learning takes place best through a combination of instructional methods reinforcing a Bible truth.

I realize that a variety of activities aids in learning,

but doesn't constant change distract from the learning process?

A lack of variation in methodology is deadly. A continuous change of the methods is also distracting to students. Variety in methodology captivates interest, but a new method does not need to be introduced every five minutes.

Over the course of a year teachers may try perhaps forty or more methods. With some they will feel comfortable; others will feel forced. Teachers will eventually settle down to a dozen or so methods that are good for them. With this variety they can make the necessary changes of pace in the classroom to insure interest, yet at the same time use methods repetitively enough to minimize distraction to the learners.

How can I encourage teachers to use a variety of methods?

Department meetings are the best place to encourage new ideas. Most published curricula give a step-by-step description of what should take place in the session. The writers of the curriculum usually try to vary the methodology used. If a teacher simply follows the lesson plans of the curriculum, he will be varying his methods.

Some programs, however, do not provide detailed lesson plans. Also, it is possible that there might be some occasions when all the methods suggested in a given lesson seem inappropriate. Teachers can substitute an alternate method, but they should be able to demonstrate to the program leader that their method would be more productive than the one published in the material.

At the department meeting the leader does not have to single-handedly convince a reluctant teacher to try new approaches to learning. Other teachers present at the meeting who practice different methods can also encourage the worker. Their attitudes at the planning session will have a modeling effect. They can also open their classrooms for a hesitant teacher to observe a typical session.

Our teachers need to realize that just as they wouldn't enjoy peanut butter and jelly three times a day, seven days a week, fifty-two weeks a year, so, too, their students would not be thrilled with an ongoing monologue week after week. It has been said that variety is the spice of life. Program leaders need to help teachers get past the inertia that keeps them from providing that spice in their classes.

What are the best methods for teaching preschool children?

Care must be given when speaking of "best" methods. A method is good when it is comfortable to the teacher and when it helps the learners. If a teacher is uncomfortable with a method, and if that medium does not communicate effectively with the learner, the method might be good but not for that teaching-learning situation.

Young children are active; they are curious; they are excited about investigating and manipulating their ever expanding world. For this reason *learning centers* can be effective with preschoolers. Many methods can be incorporated into the learning center concept. For example, if the lesson theme is God's creation, wooden puzzles of animals or nature can be used at one table, while a tripod magnifying glass can be set on the floor in another area to study leaves, rocks or pine cones. At another table there may be a coloring project, while at a fourth, children work with homemade playdough. The selection of

135

activities used in the learning centers should follow the suggestions in the teacher's manual, or be determined by the ministry team at their monthly meeting. The learning center approach allows students to move among the centers. Since the same Bible theme is designed into all the activities, the child is prepared for the Bible story regardless of the centers in which he chooses to participate.

Guided conversation is an important technique for working with young children. Housekeeping can be ordinary play or Christian instruction. The difference is in what the teacher says while the student is involved in the activity. When a child presses his hand in some clay, for example, the teacher may suggest that another child also make a hand print. Since the hand prints will be slightly different, the teacher can observe: "Do you notice how your hand, Tom, is different from Carrie's hand? Isn't it neat how God made each one of us different and special!" At the puzzle table a child may have just completed putting a chicken in its proper place. That in itself will offer the child a sense of accomplishment, but the insightful teacher can take the activity one step further by asking, "Kevin, do you ever eat eggs? Do you like milk? God gives us eggs from chickens (teacher points to chicken), and He gives us milk from cows (pointing to cow). Let's pray right now and thank God for all the good food he gives us."

Music is another vehicle for communicating Bible truth. Some of the methods include songs, rhymes with finger plays, or the use of rhythm instruments. Many adults vividly remember their days grinding the sand paper blocks, clanging the cymbals, or hitting the triangle bell (my favorite!). A piano or guitar can be used for accompaniment, or songs can be prerecorded on a cassette player. Perhaps the best type of music, however, is the spontaneous song led by a teacher sensitive to what is happening in the class.

Story telling is intriguing to young children. In fact, notice how even adults are more attentive as the pastor illustrates with a story than when he gives a prolonged exposition. A story can be told using the figures provided in a teacher's resource, but it can also be told on a chalkboard. Children also enjoy helping a teacher place flannel figures on a story board. Some children like sitting in a small group to hear a story told from a Bible picture book. Some teachers speak through puppets, while others like to use the overhead projector. All these methods lend themselves well to communicating Bible truth.

What are some good methods for teaching primaries and juniors?

Primaries and juniors will also benefit from some of the methods mentioned above, however, their older age gives them a greater sophistication, a longer attention span, and a boredom with things that are too trite. *Role playing* is a good example to illustrate the difference. In the preschool department, a story could be acted out with the aid of "people posters." Fabric is glued to cardboard figures to make them look like Bible characters. As the children slip their heads and arms through appropriate holes, they are ready to role play the story of the disciples following Jesus.

Juniors are more self-conscious, though. Some might feel the people posters are silly and embarrassing, but most will participate if the scene is appropriate. For example, it is not too hard to find three boys to role play a disagreement at a ball game. In response to two fellows arguing, a peacemaker could intervene, illustrating the attitude and behavior taught in the Sunday School lesson.

Another good technique for children is the combination of *story telling* with *investigative Bible study*. As children develop in their reading skills, they can be encouraged to take the initiative in the story presentation. A teacher may question: "How did David feel when he heard Goliath insulting God? What do we learn from verse 26?" The teacher's presentation and the student's investigations combine to make this technique challenging for children.

Bible games and *Bible learning activities* are also fun ways for children to learn. While Bible games are useful for teaching (i.e. Denarii, Bible Trivia, Bible Challenge), teachers can create their own games with questions drawn from the lesson or unit of study for Bible Jeopardy, Bible Password, Bible Football, or Bible Tic-Tac-Toe.

In a similar fashion, Bible Learning Activities can also be tailored to the content of a lesson. Key words of a verse can be hidden in a page of letters. Each word of a memory verse can be placed on 3 x 5 index cards and then given to a student or small group to unscramble. Children can be asked to reassemble a puzzle made by mounting a story picture on cardboard and cutting it into pieces.

Many children enjoy *art projects*. A Bible scene can be reconstructed in a diorama using a shoe box, dirt, sand, rocks, and pipe cleaners for figures. Primaries may enjoy sponge painting, soap painting or vegetable printing. Papier-mache, mosaics, mobiles or cartooning may be preferred by juniors.

As children's vocabularies increase, *creative writing* assignments can be used to enhance learning. Children can write a paragraph summarizing a Bible account, or write a short letter to a real or imaginary friend about one aspect of the Bible lesson.

Children enjoy discovery and appreciate variety. Many creative methods are available to teachers who work with first through sixth graders.

Which methods will involve teenagers without

making them self-conscious?

Adolescents are both children and adults. Sometimes we are bothered by their immaturity, yet on other occasions we are amazed at their insights or the way they assume responsibility. Acceptance is very important to teens. Peer pressure is ever present among junior and senior highs. A variety of methods can be used with teens, but care should be given not to embarrass an individual, or to allow a group's contribution to be ridiculed.

Young people prefer *interaction methods* over a lecture. When a group first comes together, the teacher may need to initiate the interaction through a question and answer format. Perhaps an agree/disagree question might be asked, allowing students to share why they made their particular choice. As group members become comfortable with one another, however, good questions will elicit discussion among the students themselves.

The *problem solving* method, especially when it is used in small groups, involves the class in the learning process, too. In this method group members work together to suggest solutions to a problem, and then assess their alternatives. After selecting their best solution, each group reports its findings to the whole class. Case studies and inductive Bible studies can also be assigned to small groups with each group sharing their results.

The *research and report* method is also profitable when working with young people. Whether the assignment is given to an individual or to a team of teens, the research and report method adds minutes and hours to the learning session through the students' out-of-class preparation. The teens may be assigned the project of asking a pastoral staff member about the meaning of baptism. They may survey friends at school as to what they believe is important in life. Some may be asked to explain a Bible text after some research in the church library. A student may report on a significant book that parallels the course theme.

The research and report method does not exempt the teacher from serving as the catalyst for learning. During the week the teacher should call his students to encourage them with their projects. These out-of-class methods, along with the many in-class methods suggested in a teacher's manual, help teens learn in relevant ways the timeless truths of Scripture.

Without getting into childish activities, how can teachers include adults in the learning process?

Most adults attend Sunday School by choice. Some may participate because of the desire of their spouse or because they want to demonstrate a good example to their children. But if an adult does not enjoy his Bible class, he will usually stop attending. While some adults have been taught to be passive in the learning process, good teaching methods will help them take responsibility for their learning, and challenge them into greater involvement.

Because of the poor quality of many lectures, some people believe that the lecture method should be abandoned. However, the *lecture* method is not a bad means of instruction. A lecture can communicate a large amount of material in a relatively short period of time. Combined with other methods and supported with illustrations and visuals, this method can be especially effective. It is important for a teacher who uses the lecture method to remember that he is teaching students, though, not primarily a content. The subject must be communicated with good eye contact and learner involvement.

It is generally true that the best method for teaching adults is *discussion*. As friends meet together in a home, it is natural for everyone to share in the conversation. The question and answer method centers the dialogue between the teacher and pupil whereas the discussion method permits the communication to move among all of the class members. Circular seating enhances discussion, and where a group is large, semi-circular seating is better than straight rows. A combination of mini-lectures and discussion provides a good balance of impression and expression.

Small groups in the form of diads, triads or more can be used during part of the class to discuss a particular passage or related issue. Group assignments should be well thought out by the leader. Instructions to the group may be listed on a sheet of paper or shown on an overhead screen. After the small group has completed its study, a spokesperson from the group should report their findings to the whole class.

The same information presented in a lecture can be discovered in a small group. The advantage of the small group, however, is that the students are more directly involved with the passage. In addition, class members will experience the by-product of fellowship (the developing of supportive relation-ships) which seldom occurs during a lecture.

In the *inductive Bible study* method the class is primarily concerned with three questions: "What does the text say?" "What does the text mean?" and "How does that apply to Christians living in the twentieth century?" Too often people seek applications from a passage before studying the textual meaning. A study of the words in a particular Bible portion, and their grammatical relationship to one another, will produce an understanding of what has been said. Second, interpreting the text will become easier when we know who and to whom the passage was given; when and where it was recorded; and why the author was writing. The third step in the inductive method is the making of personal application.

Many other methods can also be used effectively with adults, just as there are scores of methods that can be used with children and teens. A chart of Selected Teaching Methods is given at the end of the chaper.

Summary

If a football team repeated the same play on every down, the opposition would soon stop that play, and probably throw the team for a loss. A good offensive team varies its plays. It uses passes and runs; traps and sweeps; the quick out and the bomb. The diversity of plays keeps the team moving; and when the plays are used in an effective combination, a score will result.

Using a combination of methods will also enhance the teaching/learning process. Changes of pace in the classroom help learners become successful in their understanding of the Bible. As a teacher varies his or her methodology, students will score in mastery learning.

SELECTED TEACHING METHODS

Method	Preschool	Children	Youth	Adults
Agree - Disagree			x	x
Book Reports		x	x	x
Brainstorming		x	x	x
Buzz Groups			x	x
Case Studies			x	x
Chalkboard		x	x	x
Charts		x	x	x
Circle Response			x	x
Choral Reading		x	x	

Method	Preschool	Children	Youth	Adults
Crayon Etching or Rubbing	x	x		
Creative Writing		x	x	
Debates				x
Dioramas	x	x		
Diary		x	x	
Discussion		x	x	x
Displays		x	x	x
Dramatization	x	x	x	x
Field Trips	x	x	x	
Films, Filmstrips, Slides	x	x	x	x
Flannelgraph	x	x	x	
Friezes	x	x	x	
Hymn Writing		x	x	
Inductive Study		x	x	x
Interview		x	x	x
Lecture				x
Maps	x	x	x	x
Memorization		x	x	
Murals		x	x	
Neighbor Nudging			x	x
Object Lessons	x	x		

Method	Preschool	Children	Youth	Adults
Open End Stories		x	x	
Outlining			x	x
Painting (string, sponge, etc.)	x	x		
Pantomine		x	x	
Paper Bag Puppets	x	x		
Paraphrasing			x	x
People Posters	x	x		
Pictures	x	x		
Posters		x	x	
Problem solving			x	x
Projects		x	x	x
Puppets	x	x	x	
Puzzles	x	x		
Question and Answer			x	x
Question Box			x	x
Quiz		x	x	
Reports		x	x	x
Review	x	x	x	x
Role Playing	x	x	x	x
Singing	x	x	x	x
Skits			x	x

Method	Preschool	Children	Youth	Adults
Storytelling	x	x	x	x
Surveys		x	x	x
Testimonies			x	x
Time Line		x	x	x
Word Associations		x	x	x
Writing a Prayer		x	x	x

RESOURCES FOR METHODS

Accent Teacher Training Series. (5 Books, see Teacher Training resources). Denver: Accent Publications, 1979-1981.

Benson, Clarence H. *Teaching Techniques.* Wheaton: ETTA, 1974.

Bolton, Barbara. *Creative Bible Learning for Children.* Glendale, CA: International Center for Learning, 1977.

Bolton, Barbara and Smith, Charles T. *Bible Learning Activities.* Ventura, CA: Regal Books, 1973.

Ford, Leroy. *A Primer for Teachers and Leaders.* Nashville, TN: Broadman Press, 1963.

Ford, Leroy. *Design for Teaching and Training.* Nashville, TN: Broadman Press, 1978.

Galloway, Chester O. *Team Teaching With Adults.* Kansas City: Beacon Hill Press, 1972.

Gangel, Kenneth. *24 Ways To Improve Your Teaching.* Wheaton: Victor Books, 1974.

Getz, Gene A. *Audio Visual Media in Christian Education.* Chicago: Moody Press, 1972.

Johnson, Rex and Reed, Bobbie. *Bible Learning Activities—Youth.* Ventura, CA: Regal Books, 1974.

LeFever, Marlene D. *Turnabout Teaching.* Elgin, IL: David C. Cook Publishing Company, 1973.

Leypoldt, Martha M. *40 Ways to Teach in Groups.* Valley Forge: Judson Press, 1967.

Marlowe, Monroe and Reed, Bobbie. *Creative Bible Learning For Adults.* Glendale: International Center for Learning, 1977.

McDaniel, Elsiebeth and Richards, Lawrence O. *You and Preschoolers.* Chicago: Moody Press, 1975.

Pearson, Mary Rose. *Bible Object Lessons.* Denver: Accent Publications, 1991.

Pearson, Mary Rose. *More Bible Object Lessons.* Denver: Accent Publications, 1992.

Richards, Lawrence O. *You and Adults.* Chicago: Moody Press, 1974.

Teaching Techniques. Wheaton, IL: ETTA, 1974.

7

PREPARING THE BALL FIELD: Facilities

One night the pro football team in our town played their third preseason game. The next afternoon a game was scheduled for the professional baseball team. Overnight the grounds keepers transformed the field from a long, rectangular surface with horizontal lines and hash marks, to a diamond shaped arena with two long lines, bases and a mound.

Whether the game is soccer, football or baseball, the quality of the play is related to the condition of the field, Similarly, in the game of Christian education, the better the facilities the easier it will be for the teaching team to perform well.

What is a good teaching facility?

A good teaching facility is one that enhances the learning process. An elaborate, super-equipped facility is not essential. A busy classroom can hinder learning just as much as a barren classroom. A good learning environment does not call attention to itself, but quietly complements the teacher's work with the students.

An effective teaching environment is clean and cheerful. It minimizes visual and auditory distractions. It allows students enough space for personal involvement in the learning process, but is not so large it sidetracks their interest from activities. Learning aids in a good classroom should be easily accessible to both the teacher and the students.

A classroom at the church becomes a home away from home. For the preschooler, it is that secure place of love and affection; for the child, it is that familiar place of acceptance and growth; for the teenager, it is a comfort zone for the testing of values and the building of relationships; and for the adult, it is a center for Biblical instruction and fellowship. From books and bulletin boards to carpets and coffee, a well-equipped classroom helps students feel welcome in their place of learning.

How do we determine how much space we need for our church's educational program?

While many schools function well with less than an ideal amount of space, square footage recommendations are available as a general guide. Because young children learn through play, their classrooms should have enough space for learning centers and sufficient room in which to move around. Children and teens need slightly less space per pupil because most of their activities are in large or small groups. Adults can function with the least amount of space, especially where large group lecture or discussion is predominant. A teaching arrangement that seats class members around tables necessitates double the amount of space.

The square footage suggestions below are determined by age-level teaching methodology:

Early Childhood (2-Kindergarten):   30-35 Sq. Ft. Per Pupil
Children (Grades 1-6):   25-30 Sq. Ft. Per Pupil
Youth (Grades 7-12):   20-25 Sq. Ft. Per Pupil
Adults (College age and up)   10-20 Sq. Ft. Per Pupil

The square footage requirements above assume that classroom space is not used for extraneous storage. Cluttered rooms are aesthetically unattractive, and they hinder the usefulness of a facility. Old dressers or other furniture which take up valuable floor space, for example, should be replaced with wall mounted cupboards. A well-planned room will maximize its space to help the learners for whom it was designed.

What equipment is needed in the classroom?

A *nursery* must provide cribs, changing table(s), cupboards, diapers, washcloths and linens. Other useful equipment includes a sink, toilet, a refrigerator for milk or juice, a washable area rug, adult rocking chairs, baby swings, scrubbable toys, Bible picture books, a separate, private space for nursing mothers, and a stereo or cassette player.

Preschool Departments (2's - 5's) will need low tables and chairs for learning centers, and a story rug for group time. Cabinets for storing blocks, puzzles and table games can double as dividers between learning centers. Bulletin boards and chalkboards should be mounted twenty inches from the floor. A record player, dress-up clothes (for a home living center), and materials for a God's Wonders Center will all enhance the classroom.

The *Primary (Grades 1-2), Middler (Grades 3-4), and Junior (Grades 5-6) Departments* will also need tables and chairs, chalkboards and tackboards. A tack strip for displaying the students' work should be mounted thirty-two inches from the floor. Storage and book cabinets for materials, Bibles and reference books are beneficial. Some classrooms may have a piano, and all will profit form Bible maps on flip charts or on transparencies.

Teens and adults need classrooms that offer flexibility. Learning activities may be in large groups, small groups circled in chairs, or groups of students seated at tables. Chalkboards, screens, or other displays should be placed forty inches from the floor. A lectern and overhead projector should be available for regular use. A refreshment table is convenient for those classes that begin with an informal coffee time.

How important is kid-sized furniture?

Since children live in homes with adult furniture, some people argue that they do not need smaller furniture during the three hours they attend church. However, careful observation will reveal that children do spend more time in surroundings adapted to their size.

Some youngsters attend preschools which use down-sized furniture. Elementary age children spend all day at desks manufactured for their particular age. Even when children are at home, they frequently sit on the floor, or on a chair or sofa with their legs tucked under them. The height of a standard chair (designed seventeen inches from the heel to the back of the knee) is not natural for children.

When new furnishings are purchased for a room, and the facility is used mainly for a specific age, thoughtful consideration will lead to the purchase of appropriate chairs and tables. Low toilets can be ordered for the preschool bathroom. Learning center tables should have legs no higher than twenty inches. Children will more easily notice visuals that are displayed at their own height.

Chairs are manufactured beginning at six inches, and increasing in two inch increments to the adult size of sixteen to seventeen inches. While some schools may desire exact sized chairs for each age group, most can function smoothly with ten inch chairs for preschoolers, fourteen inch chairs for children, and seventeen inch chairs for youth and adults. If a school prefers to only purchase two sizes of chairs, a good combination is twelve inch chairs for the younger grades, and sixteen inch chairs for the older grades and adults.

Tables should be set ten inches higher than the chairs in a classroom. For example, a class that uses fourteen inch chairs for their juniors, will want table heights of twenty-four inches. Although more expensive initially, tables with adjustable legs offer a flexibility that may prove less expensive in the long run.

A Christian education facility that provides two or three sizes of chairs, tables with adjustable legs, and visual boards at the learners' level is well on the way to maximizing the effect of a learning environment that will help students feel comfortable in their study of the Bible.

How should classrooms be arranged to facilitate learning?

We said previously that preschoolers learn through a world of play; children learn through Bible activities and games; youth learn through small group interaction; and adults learn primarily through discussion. Room arrangements should complement those learning methods.

The early childhood classroom should have enough space to allow movement by the child. If learning centers are used, the room arrangement for preschoolers should include several round (or kidney shaped) tables separated by cabinets or portable dividers to create a variety of places to study. By locating these centers at the perimeter of the room, or at one end of a room, a separate area is maintained for story telling and group activities.

Primaries and juniors also benefit from classrooms that are arranged for small group and large group activities. Clusters of eight to ten children with their teachers can be positioned in the corners of a classroom. Tables will aid their Bible study, writing and handwork.

If there are more than ten children in an age group, subdividing the classes is profitable. However, because of the competition factor of sound distractions, three or four groups work better than two classes. For instance, three classes of six children will be more compatible than two classes of eight children. While this will necessitate another teacher, the noise factor of the three groups will actually be less distracting than the competition of the two. Even with the best of dividers, the story telling or instruction of one teacher will naturally draw away the attention of some students from the second group.

While most of the teaching in the childhood division will take place in small groups, students will still come together for review of the story, music or the presentation of projects. Since few schools are able to afford two chairs per pupil, the assembly time should be near the center of the room where pupils can regroup with the least amount of confusion.

When it comes to youth rooms, it seems that almost anything goes! Some high school groups meet in the church basement where the teens have been allowed to paint murals on the walls and furnish the area to their preference. Some youth groups have been given the upper floor of an educational building where a stereo and plenty of contemporary Christian music precedes and follows the teaching sessions. One senior high room was equipped with air hockey, ping-pong and bumper pool; another group laid claim to an old garage and converted it to their personal preference. However, many groups meet in conventional classrooms.

A youth room should be large enough to allow teens to study in both large and small groups, and also to mix and talk informally with one another. A couple of work tables are good for writing projects and reports or for making collages and posters for learning activities. A centralized teaching area with a screen for visual media instruction is also important. While young people will often meet in small groups, reports and instruction are more easily followed from an end of a room where attention can be centrally focused.

The arrangement of an adult classroom will vary with the number of adults in attendance. A chalkboard or overhead projector will probably be used frequently by the adult teacher, so a configuration which brings students around the teacher will enhance the learning process. A dozen adults may enjoy sitting in a circle. When the teacher joins them in the circle, he can participate both as a group member (during discussion) and as a leader (during lecture).

The circular arrangement loses its effectiveness beyond seventeen members, though. The group dynamics, such as freedom to share personal concerns, will decrease as the group gets larger. For groups numbering over eighteen, semi-circular seating will draw people close to the teaching center, yet permit them to face each other during discussion. If buzz groups are desired, chairs may be circled for subgroupings. Again, three or four groups work better than two in order to avoid individual, competing voices.

Where space permits, tables are a nice feature in adult classrooms. On the flat surface of a table the adult can open his Bible, use a study guide sheet, and even put his coffee. In addition, sitting around a circular table draws the group members together in close proximity, yet the table keeps them from feeling on top of one another.

Should we keep teaching supplies in one central location, or should they be decentralized into each classroom?

There are two important factors regarding teaching supplies: Availability and control. Supplies must be out where the teacher can use them, but they must be controlled for the purpose of inventory and proper use. A central supply is advantageous regarding control, but decentralization has the advantage of making the supplies handy to the teachers. Churches that have a problem getting materials to the teacher may want to try placing frequently used supplies in each classroom. Sunday Schools that have trouble with control may prefer a centralized location. Local factors determine which procedure is best for a given education ministry.

Many churches have found it beneficial to have a central supply for a comprehensive inventory, but also to keep individual classrooms stocked with common supplies. A wall-mounted cupboard, located above a media table or other equipment, will provide ample storage. Pencils, crayons, markers, tape, art paper, glue, rulers, old magazines and other consumables can each have a location within the cabinet. This arrangement is a little harder on program leaders who have the responsibility of inventory, but it will keep the materials closer to the students who are the focus of attention.

Our room is shared with a week-day school. How can we best maintain our own identity and suitable teaching environment?

Churches and Christian schools that share facilities occasionally feel the discomfort of their joint arrangement. However, as good stewards of the resources that God has given, churches that share space can rejoice in the effective usage of their facilities. Most corporations do not construct a building that is used only three hours per week. How, then, can churches dare to convert the gifts of God's people into brick and mortar that stand idle each week day. Expanding the use of our educational rooms is wise, and careful procedures can minimize the problems of divided ownership.

Mutual respect must be practiced by both groups who share a facility. At the conclusion of class, teachers should prepare the room for the next group. However, they should also arrive early enough before their next class session in case the other staff did not reciprocate the courtesy. A custodian who knows the room arrangements of both groups can enhance the cordial relationship. A pastor, or the staff person in authority over both groups, may also have to remind both ministry teams of the equal value of both programs to the life of the church.

Some churches have solved their supply problems by maintaining separate, lockable cabinet space for each group. Bulletin boards are also divided between the school and the church teachers. Each group assumes responsibility for their own materials.

In one church, occasional resentment surfaced between the church staff and the school staff because the Sunday School teachers used the supplies of the nursery school. After trying several arrangements, the staff finally came up with a new suggestion. For one year the church and school monitored the supply expenses of the Christian education program of the church. In subsequent years, the school purchased all the supplies and maintained the inventory, but at the end of each fiscal year, the church C.E. committee reimbursed the school for their part of the supplies. The resentment over borrowing and maintaining enough supplies was minimized by this practice.

155

We are a small church and only have one building. How can we best run our educational program?

When churches plan their first building, they usually design it with flexibility in mind. Typically there is a large meeting room with classrooms either in the basement or on both sides of the assembly room. In situations like these, the multi-purpose room must be kept attractive (for it is used for worship), yet practical (because it doubles as a teaching facility). Flexibility is also important in the selection of furnishings. For example, comfortable stacking chairs can be locked together into straight rows, moved into circles, or set aside in a corner.

Where only one large room is used for several classes (especially if classes are across age divisions), distractions are a common problem. To deal with this problem, some churches have constructed sound proof, "L" shaped dividers which subdivide the large room into classrooms. After Sunday School the dividers are pushed into two corners, neatly tucked inside each other. Other churches have put hooks into the walls of their multi-purpose rooms. From these hooks chalkboards and bulletin boards are suspended during teaching hours, but prior to worship (or youth fellowship, special dinners, or weddings), the boards are lifted off the hooks, placed on a cart, and rolled into a storage area.

Regardless of what size church, every fellowship needs to maximize its facility usage. One church had a large sanctuary, but inadequate Christian education space. Under the leadership of a new pastor, they framed in two large classrooms in the rear of the auditorium, providing additional educational space and bringing the people closer together for worship. This church has already decided to offer double worship services when growth necessitates a change, but if the larger auditorium were needed, reconversion of the sanctuary could easily be accomplished.

Growing churches often struggle with space problems, but these problems are signs of life. Some churches have tried to solve their problems by bringing portable classrooms onto the church site. Some fellowships place classes in the homes of members who live near the church. Where the only facility available to the congregation is their one building, though, flexible seating with movable partitions is essential.

Is there any benefit in renting facilities or using facilities away from our church campus?

Facilities are not sacred. It is the message of the Scriptures that is sacred, and our goal is the teaching of that message to people. There is nothing wrong with renting facilities or meeting away from the church campus. A youth group may use the family room of a nearby home, or a singles class may use the banquet room of a restaurant. In fact, the atmosphere of the restaurant is a great halfway situation where unchurched people may be more willing to study the Bible.

Sensitivity must be given to which groups are located off campus. Senior highs, singles or young marrieds without children are better choices for relocation than first graders or senior citizens.

Since the nursery and children's classes are best located near the sanctuary, supplemental classes should be located close to the church so that valuable time is not wasted in travel. Using facilities near the church property is economical; it offers a more relaxed atmosphere for learning, and a good strategy for reaching out to the unchurched.

I heard that some churches use their facilities in double or triple sessions. How does this work?

When space becomes a problem, the quickest and least expensive solution is to use the facility twice. Many churches have accommodated an increase of worshippers by offering an 8:30 a.m. and 11:00 a.m. service, with a 9:45 Sunday School in between. This arrangement doubles the seating of the sanctuary, but does not enlarge the educational space.

When additional space is needed in both worship and Sunday School, many churches have adopted a "double session" schedule. In the double session arrangement, two identical worship services are conducted at 9:45 and at 11:00 a.m. While each of the two worship services are being conducted, Sunday School classes run concurrently.

Sunday Schools over 500 usually have enough students to offer two sections of each learning group (i.e. primaries or young marrieds at both the first and second hours). Adults may have a choice of electives either hour, or a stage-graded class either hour.

Smaller churches that need double sessions but do not have enough people to offer each age group a choice of study hours, predetermine which hour classes will meet. The worship service in which people participate will therefore be regulated by which hour they attend Sunday School. A careful scheduling of adult stage-graded classes, or the offering of electives, will assure parents the possibility of participating with their younger children in worship.

An example of the double session arrangement is given at the end of the chapter. In the schedule, the junior high department meets at the 9:30 hour for Sunday School and then for worship at 11:00 a.m. The senior highs first attend worship, and then use the same youth room for their study hour. Both the sanctuary and the classroom double their usage in this plan.

The key to moving into a double session schedule is good planning and thorough communication. One church began in June to publicize their new fall schedule. It began by emphasizing the need for, and the benefits of, the double sessions. In each monthly newsletter, it answered typical questions that were asked about the new format. The promotional information that this church used is also included at the end of this chapter.

I heard of a church that uses an observation room in their C.E. program. How does this work?

Very few churches can afford the space to build an observation room, but where this type of facility is possible, it offers several benefits. One church I visited had two classrooms separated by a 10'x20' observation room. Two-way glass mirrors were built into the walls between the classrooms and the observation room. People in the observation room could see what was happening in either classroom, but the students saw only the mirrors.

This type of facility can be used in many ways. Program leaders can observe both teachers and students, and use their observations to offer commendations and suggestions for the classroom activities. Leaders can also use the room for prospective teachers to study master teachers prior to assuming their own classrooms. Dads and moms may observe a three-year-old class, noting how a teacher uses guided conversation in directing the child's thoughts toward spiritual things. Parents and teachers can also develop a strategy to help a child with a behavioral problem. The school and parent join as partners in the learning process, and most parents would be eager to help their child who demonstrates a special need.

Churches that cannot afford a special room for observation

can still place 4' x 4' two-way glass mirrors between two of their classrooms. During regular class use, curtains can cover the mirrors. An observation room is available when needed, however, by simply reassigning one of the classes or perhaps combining for the day with another group.

We are thinking of constructing a new educational building. What suggestions might you give us regarding its design?

Many books provide details for classroom arrangements and give square footage requirements. An education building should not just provide adequate space, however. It should also follow a master plan. Rather than building simply to increase C.E. space, an architect familiar with church construction can prepare a design which is complementary to the worship, fellowship and evangelism purposes of the church.

A master plan will minimize foreseeable problems. One church began their building program near the rear of their property, anticipating their final sanctuary position at the corner/intersection. In subsequent years, however, they learned that their township would not grant them a building permit because they did not have enough green belts and parking. An architect can help avoid these kinds of problems by helping with building codes and special requirements, as well as by designing a building that will be aesthetically pleasing and functionally efficient.

A second suggestion regarding construction is to plan as much flexibility into your building as is affordable. One church in California constructed a five story education building without any internal bearing walls. The inside wall sections move on tracks in the floor and ceiling and they have a high sound barrier rating. While this type of facility is financially out of range for most churches, the principle of flexibility in construction is important.

Another church built a Christian education wing that had four 30′ x 30′ classrooms with internal bearing walls. A few years later they changed the groups assigned to those classrooms. When they realized that 900 sq. ft. rooms were not essential for their new ministry, they wished they had six 20′ x 30′ rooms (600 sq. ft.) rather than the larger four rooms. If the internal walls were non-bearing studs and sheet rock (or better yet, collapsible walls), they could have made the internal adjustment, and had an additional two rooms.

One last comment is in order. A factor that is sometimes overlooked in the planning phase of a building program is that furnishings will cost 10-15 percent of the overall expense of a new building. These furnishing costs must be planned into a project for a realistic picture of the overall building expenses.

Summary

A number of year ago I was playing softball on a church team. On one occasion I moved in to grab a ball on the first hop when to my surprise the ball took a twenty foot hop, going over my head, and rolling to the fence. Each fall the field was used for football and the yard lines were cut into the grass. While the etching process allowed the recreation department to easily chalk the field, it did not help the fly ball that landed on the edge of a line during our playoff game.

That game was not won or lost, however, on that particular play. Neither is the game of Christian education won or lost on the condition of one or two classrooms. Some things we are not able to alter in our facilities, but there may be some simple changes (such as the timely application of a gallon of paint) that can help our learners week after week.

SAMPLE DOUBLE SESSION SCHEDULE

MORNING SCHEDULE FOR WORSHIP AND EDUCATION

Trinity Church provides two identical worship services. The same Bible message, choir anthem, and special music are given at both the 9:30 and 11:00 hours.

The educational program runs concurrently with the worship hours with some classes meeting at 9:30 and others at 11:00.

If you attend worship only, you may choose either the early service or the late service. If you attend Bible School and Worship, your worship hour will be determined by the scheduled time of your Bible Class. You will attend worship the opposite hour that your class meets.

All adult classes will be studying the Gospel of John. If you have a conflict with the hour your class is scheduled (i.e. your children's schedule), feel free to choose a class the alternate hour.

AGE GROUP	*TIME OF BIBLE CLASS*	*LOCATION*
Cribbers & Toddlers	9:30 - 12:05	Nursery
2½ & 3 year olds	9:30 - 12:05	Lower Auditorium, #3
4 & 5 year olds	9:30 - 12:05	Lower Auditorium, #2
1st Grade	11:00	Lower Auditorium, #1
2nd Grade	11:00	Youth Building
3rd Grade	11:00	Administration, 2nd Flr.
4th Grade	11:00	Administration, 2nd Flr.
5th Grade	11:00	Fell. House, 2nd Flr.
6th Grade	11:00	Administration, 3rd Flr.
Junior High	11:00	Administration, 3rd Flr.
Senior High	9:30	Administration, 3rd Flr.
S.A.L.T. (Singles)	9:30	Fell. House, 1st Flr.
Young Adults	9:30	Fell. House, Lvg. Rm.
Homebuilders	11:00	Fell. House, Garage
Reapers	11:00	Fell. House, Lvg. Rm.
Ambassadors	9:30	Fell. House, Garage

One church adopted a double session schedule mainly because of space needs during worship. Notice that the children's classes are scheduled at 11:00 a.m., necessitating the first session worship for the children and their parents. The arrangement was intentional by the leadership to regulate sanctuary attendance. Since most visitors, and adults who did not participate in Sunday School, primarily worshipped at 11:00 a.m., the flexibility of double sessions allowed a balancing of sanctuary worship.

PROMOTION OF DOUBLE SESSIONS

The information which follows was used by one church to promote a change in their Sunday morning programming. The questions and answers appeared in their newsletter (three questions in June and three in July). The church moved into the new schedule after Labor Day, and has maintained the double session format, even after three building campaigns.

Starting Sunday, September 3, 1972, Trinity Church will begin the popular two worship service and two Sunday School schedule for services. The 2+2 (as it is often called) will offer worship services at 9:45 a.m. and 11:00 a.m., with Sunday School classes also at 9:45 a.m. and 11:00 a.m. Much time, study, consideration and planning was spent by the Christian Education Committee and the Board of Deacons regarding our church's needs and possible arrangements to meet those needs. In light of this study, the 2+2 has been adopted.

2+2 QUESTIONS ANSWERED

WHAT IS THE 2+2?

The 2+2 is a total Sunday morning program which offers two

163

worship services and two Sunday Schools running concurrently. People will either go to Sunday School and then church (as they presently do), or they will go to church, then Sunday School.

The order in which you attend Sunday School and church will depend on the Sunday School class to which you belong or the elective classes which you choose.

WHY DO WE NEED THE 2+2?

We need the 2+2 for two main reasons: (1) the additional space it will give us for Sunday School classes, and (2) the improvement in quality it will offer to our worship services and Bible classes.

As good stewards of the property that God has entrusted to us, the 2+2 will use most of our classrooms twice on Sunday mornings instead of only once. For example, the large room off the kitchen will be used at 9:45 a.m. by the Junior High Dept. (while the Junior Dept. is in church), and then at 11:00 a.m. by the Junior Dept. (while the Junior Highs are in church).

The quality of our worship services will also increase with the beginning of the 2+2. The Morning Worship (9:45 and 11:00) will be identical—both will have the same choir, special music and other parts of the service. This will be a real improvement over last year's 8:30 a.m. service. Teachers and other educational workers will also enjoy serving under the 2+2, since they will no longer always have to miss either their Sunday School class or the worship service.

ARE THERE ANY ALTERNATIVES TO THE 2+2?

When a church is as fortunate as ours to see a God-blessed increase of over 20% per year, who can help but rejoice? On the other hand, as you well know, rapid growth also produces problems, especially in the areas of staffing and facility. In planning for a 3-5 year church growth, three alternatives were considered for Trinity. The *first* was to build enough buildings to adequately seat all the people at one time. This alternative has already been rejected regarding our sanctuary and classrooms. We will use them twice instead of building larger ones. We cannot afford to build three to four more educational buildings when we are not adequately using our present facilities.

The *second* alternative for increasing Sunday School space was to put classes in homes. We would need three to four homes now, and in a projected 3-5 year growth more then half of our classes would need to be in homes. For common sense reasons this alternative was rejected. It would be impossible for either parents, or the church, to run such a large scale shuttle service—the central location of the local body is essential.

The *third* alternative is the 2+2, and as you can see, a feasible solution to our growth pains. As you know, our growth plans include starting as many as three mission churches, but this will not stop Trinity's growth. We need to be prepared to meet the needs of our growing community.

WILL THE NEW PLAN SPLIT FAMILIES?

NO. Since third grade children and under are in a unified program (Sunday School and children's church), they are not in worship service anyway. The parents of Juniors and Junior Highs will, for the most part, be in the same worship service, so they could sit together if they choose. Senior Highs and Collegians rarely sit with their parents.

Another advantage of the 2+2 is that Adults will have two elective classes to choose from for each age division. Since one class will be offered each hour, there is no reason why families should be separated.

WILL CHOIR MEMBERS HAVE TO MISS SUNDAY SCHOOL CLASSES?

Since the adult choir will be singing in both worship services in the 2+2 arrangement, some are afraid they will have to miss their S.S. class. However, this is *not* the case. Beginning this fall, the choir will no longer remain in the choir loft during the entire morning service. Rather, they will be dismissed after the anthem (which will be in the first fifteen minutes of the service). Choir members whose S.S. Class meets during that hour will leave for their class, while the other members remain in the sanctuary for worship. The second service will be the same, with choir members again being dismissed to either class or worship.

DOES THE 2+2 CREATE TWO CHURCHES WITHIN ONE BUILDING?

NO! Actually, in the 2+2, nothing much changes except the double use of our facilities. Age-graded Sunday School classes will still be meeting together, and thus retain the fellowship experience with one another. The 9:45 and 11:00 times will be the same as they have been in the past, and will continue to allow time for talking with friends before, between and after the worship service/Sunday School hours.

8

MEASURING THE TEAM'S EFFECTIVENESS: Evaluation

At the beginning of a football season, professional teams are loaded with players who have reported to training camp. As the pre-season progresses, however, some players are cut and others are traded. When the regular season begins, each team will have a reduced roster of forty-five men. Managers and coaches do not make their player selection arbitrarily, but base their assessments on observations and data collected on each individual. The ultimate goal of a football club is to win the Super Bowl, and evaluations of players are made in the context of who will best help the team accomplish that goal.

In Christian education, our goal is to help people become a mirror image of Jesus Christ. Our Lord has brought us together as a team to accomplish the purposes of evangelism and edification. We strive for a prize that is far more valuable than a Super Bowl ring, therefore it is important for those involved in an educational ministry to strive for excellence. Evaluation is an essential process for helping us reach our goal.

Why should we use evaluation in our Christian education program?

I remember, as a child, steering the outboard motor on my cousin George's boat as we crossed Lake Elizabeth. George told me, "See that house on the other side, Johnny? Just keep steering toward it." As we traveled across the lake there were times when I had to turn to the right, or to the left, in order to keep the boat on target. Those adjustments were made because I could see that I was drifting off course. Because of the assessments, I was able to arrive at our destination and accomplish the goal of docking the boat on the other side of the lake.

Unfortunately, few people in Christian ministry think about evaluation, and even fewer people regularly practice it. Some individuals have the attitude that it is unspiritual to measure a pastor's performance or a Sunday School teacher's class session. However, even Jesus practiced evaluation. He would often teach His disciples, and then send them out to test their learning. He would give them a lesson on faith, and then ask them to cross a lake, knowing full well a storm would arise to test that faith. In fact, one day every individual will stand before Jesus as He assesses the faithfulness of believers, or as He judges the ungodly.

Evaluation is essential to let us know how we are doing. A golfer's score is an evaluation of his play on a given day; a dieter's weight is an assessment of progress on a new weight loss program; and a salesman's commissions reveal the degree to which he has successfully distributed his product. Measurement is a way of life. Very few enterprises endure through time without the systematic measuring of their effectiveness.

What an unfortunate contrast is found in the church. Pastors may preach and shepherd year after year without the guidance of evaluation. Deacons may continually be voted to the church board without ever weighing their value to the leadership. A youth sponsor may work unassisted for years with a youth group, not because he is particularly effective with the teens, but because no one else will do the job.

Only a naive person would believe that our educational teams are doing the best jobs of which they are capable. But if they are not the most effective in service, in what areas do they need to improve? This question can only be answered through regular evaluation.

Exactly what should be evaluated in our Christian education ministry?

Three concerns should receive regular assessment: facility, program and staff. The least resistance to evaluation is encountered with facilities; greater resistance regarding program; and the greatest amount of apprehension in relation to teacher evaluations.

Church members often make comments about the *facilities.* Whether based on objective data, or a subjective complaint about the setting of the air-conditioning, facility assessment is relatively easy to undertake. It is not difficult to determine the amount of square footage needed for both present Sunday School enrollment, and a five-year projected enrollment. It is also fairly easy to compare the items in a classroom to a checklist of recommended equipment. Raising the necessary finances for a new education unit may prove difficult, but determining the need for an addition is much easier. From the cleanliness of a rug in the toddler room, to the availability of overhead projectors in adult clases, regular facility evaluations should be made by program leaders and the Christian Education committee.

The second concern of evaluation relates to *program.* Making assessments of this type are a little harder because they tend to be more subjective. "Should a church use Pioneer Clubs, or should they adopt the Awana program?" A simple answer to this question may be difficult because of personal preferences or local variables which have bearing upon any decision.

Rather than perpetuating a program merely because it has always been part of the church's ministry, a team can assess every program to see if it is accomplishing the stated objectives of the church. Even when a program is justified, evaluation can also reveal if it can improve in quality. For example, a Sunday School evaluation can use the assessments of both teachers and leaders. A questionnaire for evaluating the Sunday School is included in this chapter. More specifically, the strengths and weaknesses of the curriculum are measurable with the help of an evaluative tool such as the one at the end of the chapter.

"Should the youth program be moved from Wednesday evening to Thursday evening?" "Should we begin a children's church?" "Do we need a curriculum with more Bible memory work?" These and many other legitimate questions belong in the domain of program evaluation.

The most sensitive area of evaluation deals with assessing the performance of *teachers*. No one likes to be criticized, and very few people will voluntarily put themselves in a place where they might be evaluated. Since teaching staffs are comprised of volunteers, most churches do not even attempt to measure the effectiveness of their teachers. In fact, with recruitment consuming so much energy, the measurement of teacher effectiveness is frequently the last item on a leader's agenda.

Teachers do more than communicate Bible content. They themselves are the embodiment of the content. Their love for students, their commitment to preparation, the way they handle discipline, and their individualization of instruction all communicate a message. Sometimes students question the value of Sunday School. Teachers themselves sometimes wonder if they have really accomplished anything significant during the last year of their labors. Regular evaluation of the teaching staff will reveal the degree to which learning has taken place, and show additional ways teachers can grow in effectiveness.

How can a teacher assess the effectiveness of his instruction?

There are a number of means whereby a teacher can receive evaluative input.

1. A teacher can make personal assessments. After taping a class session on a cassette recorder, the teacher may ask himself several questions.
—Was there variety in the class?
—How involved were the students? Who did most of the talking?
—Did I individualize any of the instruction?
—How were instructions given; were they clear?
—How was classroom management (discipline) handled?
—What questions did the students ask? Did I understand them and answer them carefully?
—How much time was spent on the introduction, body, and conclusion of the session?
—Was adequate time left for personal application?
These questions and others can give a teacher perspective on his or her session.

2. A teacher can use evaluation forms to measure everything from preparation to actual communication in the classroom. A sample form for self-evaluation is illustrated later in this chapter. Periodically, the teacher may formulate a question-naire asking the class for input on the teaching process. It is less

threatening to talk about evaluating the "teaching-learning process" rather than the teacher. A couple of times each year students can share what they like and dislike about their classroom activities.

3. A teacher will benefit from colleague evaluations. It is profitable to have an objective third party sit in on a teacher's class session. This offers the teacher a look at the teaching process through another window. The more objective the observer, the more valuable the evaluation will be. An observation form is helpful to record data, and that information can be shared with the teacher after the class session. Forms are best left with the teacher (for referral), never kept by the observer or program leader. A sample evaluation form that has been used in several churches may also be found at the end of the chapter.

How can the threat of evaluation be minimized for teachers?

Most of us are threatened by someone evaluating our "performance." This threat can be minimized in a number of ways:

1. The church can have a comprehensive training program in which evaluation is expected of all teachers.

2. Just as attending training workshops, planning sessions, and so on is explained to teachers when they are recruited, so also the need for annual evaluations should be part of the "up front" expectations.

3. By giving immediate feedback and leaving the evaluation forms with teachers, any lingering anxiety will be minimized.

4. Encouraging teachers to mark forms graciously will not distort a teacher's profile, and it will still give direction for improvement.

5. Evaluation is less threatening to teachers working in team teaching, or in an open classroom. When a teacher is cloistered in a 10' x 10' room with her pupils, the observer is more conspicuous and distracting to all. It is better to leave small classroom doors open, or remove them from their hinges, if that is the only way a program leader can learn what is going on behind the closed doors of a classroom.

6. Let evaluation be an ongoing part of the entire church. Without bombarding the congregation with continuous surveys, seek ways to elicit input on the educational program, youth ministries, worship services, music, and even the direction and nature of the preaching.

When I pastored, the board of elders regularly assessed my performance. They provided a written summary of commendations and recommendations on each of the eleven points in my job description. Whether or not I believed the comments were one hundred percent on target did not matter. They were honest reflections on how my ministry affected the elders and our church. That information was invaluable for relevant ministry to my congregation.

If presenting "all men mature in Christ" is important, then we need to help people see that assessing our effectiveness is an imperative, spiritual task.

How can I learn more about my students and their needs?

General works on Christian education are good sources for

an overview on the general characteristics of students. Many traits of a given age group are similar because they share the same stage of life. Some publishing house materials include a section that describes age populations for whom the curriculum was written.

Even within age groupings, however, students have individual differences. Specific student information can best be gained through personal interaction with the student. A teacher may choose to use a questionnaire in class to glean information on family background or personal preferences, but the best method for gaining information about the students is to meet with them outside of class.

Several years ago I read an interesting report that documented the high value of a teacher's personal, out-of-class contact with students. The teachers that capitalized on informal moments with students were consistently ranked by the students as a "good teacher" regardless of classroom pedagogy.

If the teacher views his role as a dispenser of content, he will not have as great an effect on students as the teacher who views his role as that of the shepherd of a mini-group within the church. The good shepherd *knows* his sheep, and this is understood more quickly and thoroughly by personal relationships with students beyond the classroom.

How can we take the subjectiveness out of evaluation?

Before any function can be measured, it must first be defined. A person can identify their weight because of the increment called a "pound." He can record the temperature in a room, because "degrees centigrade" and "degrees Fahrenheit" have been predetermined. If an evaluation is nothing more than the subjective feelings of a person sitting in on a class session, the teacher will gain very little helpful input.

The greater the objectivity of the assessment, the better its use in guiding the teacher towad the improvement of instruction. Using *evaluation forms*, such as those described previously, will add validity to the evaluation process. The forms themselves are based on presuppositions of what constitutes teaching competence. Assessments made in relation to a standard offers information that is beneficial to the teacher.

Multiple observations will also minimize subjectivity in evaluation. Several observations over time, or several observations by different people, will give a more accurate picture of a teacher's classroom performance. A church using the LEROY training program, for example, will regularly have people seeking to observe and be observed as part of the certification process. It is possible that some teachers will have several colleagues ask permission to observe their class sessions. As teachers receive feedback from the evaluation forms of different observers, they can see common threads of assessment useful for their own improvement.

Conclusion

Each week professional ball clubs watch films of their previous games. The players study the films as the coaches comment on what made each play a success or a failure. Individual players will often view, for hours, their own clips or those of their opponents. For athletes, evaluation of the game is a way of life.

In the game of Christian education, however, evaluation is frequently the most absent component of a church's ministry. Yet it is evaluation that reveals whether teaching behaviors are profitable, or if they are in need of improvement. Regular evaluation of facility, program and staff will give us better direction of our energies toward our goal of conformity to the image of Christ (Romans 8:29).

SUNDAY SCHOOL EVALUATION

excellent
adequate
need improvement
poor

I. An adequate school has sufficient staff and groups to provide a good ministry to each individual person enrolled.

Questions

☐ ☐ ☐ ☐ 1. Our school has a proper ratio of teachers to students for each respective age group. One teacher for five preschool students; for elementary school years, one teacher for each six to eight students; for youth, eight to ten students; for adults, 25 to 40 students.

☐ ☐ ☐ ☐ 2. Classes are organized by appropriate ages or interests.

☐ ☐ ☐ ☐ 3. All of our staff have had an introductory course on teaching.

☐ ☐ ☐ ☐ 4. All of our staff have upgraded their teaching abilities by having some ongoing training each year.

☐ ☐ ☐ ☐ 5. The staff at our church has been, and are being recruited by means of prayer, invitation, challenge, and training.

II. An adequate school has a predominant emphasis on an evangelistic outreach.

☐ ☐ ☐ ☐ 1. The majority of the staff is currently involved in a specialized program of outreach.

☐ ☐ ☐ ☐ 2. The community is constantly made aware of our church and Sunday School by some type of media.

176

☐ ☐ ☐ ☐   3. Evangelism is constantly talked about by our staff in staff meetings and other public sessions.

☐ ☐ ☐ ☐   4. There is a sufficient variety of programming so that each person will find a happy place to study God's Word.

☐ ☐ ☐ ☐   5. Our budget allows an equal amount to be spent on outreach as is spent on the nurture of those enrolled.

excellent   *adequate*   *need improvement*   *poor*

III. An adequate school is busy making disciples.

☐ ☐ ☐ ☐   1. Each staff member is mature enough himself that he is able to disciple his students.

☐ ☐ ☐ ☐   2. Teachers spend time with their students outside the class discussing the truth taught (or students work with students).

☐ ☐ ☐ ☐   3. Students are given specific instructions on how to practice the truths taught from each unit of study.

☐ ☐ ☐ ☐   4. The pastor and the school leaders regularly spend time in prayer, personal enrichment and school planning.

☐ ☐ ☐ ☐   5. It is obvious that people in our school are loved. Our teachers give a great deal of personal attention to each student.

excellent *adequate* *need improvement* *poor*

IV. An adequate school places a high priority on a quality educational experience for each student.

☐ ☐ ☐ ☐ 1. Our school's educational experience provides for enrichment in all of the various phases—teaching, evangelism, worship, fellowship and service.

☐ ☐ ☐ ☐ 2. Our staff is developing its weekly teaching and program around one clear goal.

☐ ☐ ☐ ☐ 3. It is obvious that each teacher understands the characteristics of the age group he teaches.

☐ ☐ ☐ ☐ 4. It is obvious that each teacher understands his age group and how best to teach them.

V. An adequate school works hard to develop and maintain a sense of spiritual excellence.

☐ ☐ ☐ ☐ 1. Our whole church is caught up in praying for the school's outreach and ministry.

☐ ☐ ☐ ☐ 2. We constantly check our program to see that it is functioning according to Biblical principles.

☐ ☐ ☐ ☐ 3. Our leaders are spiritual pacesetters whose motivation and conversation is flavored by spiritual things.

☐ ☐ ☐ ☐ 4. It is obvious as you observe the staff in operation that they are not just trying to get by but that they are striving for excellence in their respective assignments.

☐ ☐ ☐ ☐ 5. A casual observation of everyone involved in the

excellent
adequate
need improvement
poor

school reveals a sense of enthusiasm toward the pupils and the program.

VI. An adequate school is guided by a pastor who is enthusiastically involved in its ministry.

☐ ☐ ☐ ☐ 1. The pastoral staff spends time on a regular basis with the superintendent in planning and prayer sessions in regard to the Sunday School.

☐ ☐ ☐ ☐ 2. The pastor takes a visible, active part in the school's teaching program.

☐ ☐ ☐ ☐ 3. The pastor is a pacesetter in evangelism, goal setting and organization.

☐ ☐ ☐ ☐ 4. The pastor is conversant with Sunday School organization and takes an active part with the leaders in its organization.

☐ ☐ ☐ ☐ 5. The pastor aids in equipping current and prospective staff for a bigger and better Sunday School.

VII. An adequate school has mobilized an effective team for the work of the ministry.

☐ ☐ ☐ ☐ 1. Each worker has been given, in writing, a clearly defined job description.

☐ ☐ ☐ ☐ 2. Lines of responsibility are set forth clearly so that each worker will be held accountable to follow through with his God-called ministry.

☐ ☐ ☐ ☐ 3. Our staff meets together both as a total unit and as individual departments for planning, communication, training and building vision.

179

☐ ☐ ☐ ☐   4. Each department works together as a team in planning and operating their department.

☐ ☐ ☐ ☐   5. Our staff is developing and following through on a yearly planning calendar of events and goals for the school.

excellent   *adequate*   *need improvement*   *poor*

VIII. An adequate school sets and works goals.

☐ ☐ ☐ ☐   1. Each one of the staff has, in writing and is clearly aware of, the specific purpose for his particular mission and how that fits into the greater goal for the Sunday School.

☐ ☐ ☐ ☐   2. Goals for the school are established by the prayer and thought processes of the majority of the team.

☐ ☐ ☐ ☐   3. Our school has discussed and recorded specific progress in relation to each goal they have established.

☐ ☐ ☐ ☐   4. The school staff has not only written out its goals but has developed a planned strategy for the fulfillment of those goals.

☐ ☐ ☐ ☐   5. Our school is willing to come with creative alternatives rather than to allow seemingly impossible roadblocks to stop them in their pursuit of fulfilling their stated objectives.

Suggested Criteria
for the
EVALUATION OF CURRICULUM MATERIALS
OF CHRISTIAN EDUCATION
in the Local Church

This suggested criteria is a simple evaluation instrument which you may use for testing the curriculum materials used in your Sunday School. The test results will help you determine if the curriculum measures up to your expectation in contributing to the achievement of the church's anticipated Christian Education goals.

Frequently workers in the local church find themselves using materials without knowing whether they fit the specific needs of that church, or even the basic needs of Bible Instruction and Christian Education.

"Yes" indicates that your selected materials may be meeting the needs of your staff and students, and thus the needs of your entire church.

	Yes	*No*
I. CONTENT VALUES:		
A. Are the aims presented in terms of expected changes in the lives of your students?	_____	_____
B. Does the material consistently help your teachers lead the students toward the experience of salvation?	_____	_____
C. Are there well-defined achievement goals, *and* is there also an emphasis on using the Bible message as a guide in decision making and problem solving?	_____	_____
D. Are the materials appropriate for the age-level understandings and physical development of the students?	_____	_____

181

	Yes	No

E. Do the student materials stimulate the pupil to use and share them with peers? (Most important as an outreach tool.) _____ _____

F. Does each unit of study arouse the curiosity and anticipation of the students? _____ _____

G. Does each lesson relate to the unit of study in a way that can be clearly understood by laymen? _____ _____

II. *TEACHER VALUES:*

A. Are the materials presented in a way that allows the teacher to absorb, understand, and teach them with a reasonable amount of preparation? _____ _____
(Professional educators recommend about 15 minutes preparation time, though if you are teaching the very young you might need much additional time.)

B. Do the materials stimulate the teacher to further self-study? _____ _____

C. Do the materials encourage and help the teacher to teach to the best of his/her ability? _____ _____

D. Do the materials help teachers decide what "must" be taught, "should" be taught, and "could" be taught? _____ _____
(Thus helping the teacher decide between the highly important, quite important, and the mildly important concepts, facts, and information.)

E. Are there "visual aids" and "tips for teaching" included with each lesson or must a teacher search through

	Yes	No

additional packets, handbooks, manuals and brochures to find the suitable helps?

F. Is there a variety of media for the teacher's use?

G. Are the teaching resources and teacher's books reusable over a two to three year period?

III. *STUDENT VALUES:*

A. Do the materials clearly present and explain activities that can be done by the student?

B. Do the materials clearly explain how salvation will help the student become committed to God, rather than only explaining about things to "do" for God?

   (To "do" something for God without being committed "to" God can produce a "donut" student. All activity on the outside with a hole in the middle.)

C. Do the materials stimulate students to study and learn more without teacher pressure?

   (Why not ask some of your students?)

D. Are the materials printed on paper that will remain usable for the full period of time expected?

E. Does the format (size of type and page design), color and art work invite the student's attention and interest?

F. Is the vocabulary selected for the age group which will use the material?

183

	Yes	No
G. Are the materials usable by students of high intelligence and alertness, or only usable by students of average intelligence and below?	___	___

IV. *TRAINING VALUES:*
   A. Do the materials include "suggestions for teaching" aimed at helping the teacher become more accomplished? ___ ___
   B. Are there teaching ideas included that are adaptable to the training of groups of teachers? ___ ___
   C. Do the "training suggestions" include both general and specific teaching ideas? ___ ___

V. *CHURCH VALUES:*
   A. Do the materials emphasize that the Sunday School is an integral part of the Church? === ===

SCORE ___ ___

Prepared by
Dr. Donald Rhodes, Assistant Superintendent,
Elementary Education, San Francisco City Schools
San Francisco, California, and Consultant in
Christian Education.

ARE YOU LEARNER CONCERNED?

Check the box which most correctly answers each of the questions below.

DO YOU ...

ALWAYS / OFTEN / SOMETIMES / SELDOM / NEVER

	ALWAYS	OFTEN	SOMETIMES	SELDOM	NEVER
PHYSICAL provide adequate lighting for reading?	☐	☐	☐	☐	☐
keep the room temperature and air circulation comfortable?	☐	☐	☐	☐	☐
arrange furnishings to encourage participation?	☐	☐	☐	☐	☐
SECURITY provide the security of a few rules that are consistently enforced?	☐	☐	☐	☐	☐
readily admit it when you don't know the answer?	☐	☐	☐	☐	☐
have an awareness of the vocabulary level of your learners?	☐	☐	☐	☐	☐
avoid using "put-downs" when opinions or ideas are different from yours?	☐	☐	☐	☐	☐
SOCIAL show a sensitivity to your learners' problems and feelings?	☐	☐	☐	☐	☐
share personal feelings and experiences in your Christian life?	☐	☐	☐	☐	☐
let Jesus love your learners through you?	☐	☐	☐	☐	☐
encourage your learners to work together?	☐	☐	☐	☐	☐

185

MEASURING THE TEAM'S EFFECTIVENESS:

		OFTEN	ALWAYS	SOMETIMES	SELDOM	NEVER

SELF-RESPECT

	OFTEN	ALWAYS	SOMETIMES	SELDOM	NEVER
plan activities that allow you to discover what your learners are really learning?	☐	☐	☐	☐	☐
see your class as individuals rather than as a group?	☐	☐	☐	☐	☐
listen to your learners?	☐	☐	☐	☐	☐
affirm your learners for sharing and cooperating in class?	☐	☐	☐	☐	☐

ACHIEVEMENT

	OFTEN	ALWAYS	SOMETIMES	SELDOM	NEVER
provide creative ways for learners to express ideas and use abilities and interests?	☐	☐	☐	☐	☐
plan a variety of learning activities during the quarter?	☐	☐	☐	☐	☐
plan ways to involve every learner?	☐	☐	☐	☐	☐

SPIRITUAL

	OFTEN	ALWAYS	SOMETIMES	SELDOM	NEVER
help your learners discover Bible truths for themselves?	☐	☐	☐	☐	☐
help your learners identify with Bible characters as real people?	☐	☐	☐	☐	☐
actively seek to discover each learner's spiritual condition and attitudes?	☐	☐	☐	☐	☐
express enthusiasm about being a Christian?	☐	☐	☐	☐	☐

Used by permission. Brown, Growe and Blankenbaker. *Teacher Training* International Center For Learning: Ventura, CA. 1982, p. 83.

EVALUATION OF THE TEACHING-LEARNING PROCESS

Realizing that this evaluation will be subjective, it will nevertheless serve as a useful tool in trying to better understand the teaching-learning process. If you feel that you are not qualified to make a judgment on an item, you may omit it.

1. A general air of FRIENDLINESS and happiness pervades the classroom

    Friendliness __:__:__:__:__ Lack of friendliness

2. ENTHUSIASM stimulates class interest

    Enthusiasm __:__:__:__:__ Lack of enthusiasm

3. The teacher uses personal examples, and is willing to admit personal shortcomings

    Honesty __:__:__:__:__ Lack of honesty

4. HUMOR in the classroom tends to promote more effective learning

    Humor __:__:__:__:__ Lack of Humor

5. Clear and commanding SPEAKING by everyone aids our learning

    Good speech __:__:__:__:__ Poor speech

6. FREEDOM FROM ANNOYANCES in the classroom contributes to the effectiveness of the teaching-learning situation

    Free from   Bothered by
    annoyances __:__:__:__:__ annoyances

7. The PROMPTNESS and efficiency of the instructor increases the value of the class

    Promptness __:__:__:__:__ Lack of promptness

187

8. The general APPEARANCE and demeanor of the teacher are appropriate

Good appearance ___:___:___:___:___ Poor appearance

9. The working relationships of the staff are complementary to each other, and add to the UNITY of the teaching-learning process.

Unity ___:___:___:___:___ Disunity

10. The teacher maintains good learning discipline in his classroom

Good discipline ___:___:___:___:___ Poor discipline

11. The purpose of the course is clear to the students

Clear purpose ___:___:___:___:___ Unclear purpose

12. The instructor's PREPARATION appears adequate

Good preparation ___:___:___:___:___ Poor preparation

13. Classroom activities are orderly and systematic

Good organization ___:___:___:___:___ Poor organization

14. ASSIGNMENTS are clear and challenging

Good assignments ___:___:___:___:___ Poor Assignments

15. Teaching methods are appropriate

Appropriate ___:___:___:___:___ Not appropriate

List methods used *)
                        *)
                        *)
                        *)
                        *)
                        *)

16. Students participate actively in class procedures

        Participate   __:__:__:__:__   Do not participate

17. The class is related to daily life

        Applicable   __:__:__:__:__   Not applicable

18. Outlines, syllabi, summaries, and other supplementary materials contribute to student learning

        Aids, materials   __:__:__:__:__   Lack of materials

19. Sufficient time is provided for REVIEW

        Review time   __:__:__:__:__   No review time

20. Does the teacher really LISTEN to his students?

        Listens   __:__:__:__:__   Does not really listen

21. The objectives of the teacher were reached

        Objectives   Objectives not
          reached   __:__:__:__:__   reached
Ask ahead of time and see if you think he reached them during the class.

22. The spiritual tone of the class

        Highly spiritual   __:__:__:__:__   Purely secular

23. The authority in the classroom was

        Word of God   __:__:__:__:__   Teacher

Name of Evaluator: _____   Date: _____

CONCLUSION

I once heard a friend say: "It sure would be fun to play baseball for a living." As he looked at the grass on the other side of the fence, he would have preferred a paycheck from sports rather than from his work at the factory.

On the surface it might appear that big leaguers have it easy— all they do is play games. Yet those familiar with professional sports know the rigors of training camp, the repetition of daily drills, the bodily wear of competition, and the fatigue caused by thousands of miles of travel each season. Athletes *do* enjoy their work, but they also *work hard* to make their play effective.

As leaders in the church we also have an enjoyable job; we are managers in the game of Christian Education. We are responsible for recruiting players, and then training them to be winners. The quality of our organization, programs, curricula, methods and facilities will directly affect the success of our team in leading students into Christlikeness.

Good team play begins with good coaching. As we continue to work hard and manage well, we will enjoy each new season the Owner gives us to coach His teams.

INDEX

INDEX

INDEX

Supplies, 154
Support of church
  ministries, 14
Supporting teachers, 26

Tables, 149
Talent survey, 28
Teachable, 12
Teacher contract, 47
Teacher evaluation, 169-175,
  185-189
Teacher job description, 15,
  36-46
Telling stories, 136
Threat of evaluation, 172
Tenure of service, 16
Term of service, 16,47
Testing, 104
Training, 111-131
Two Plus Two, 158,162-166
Two Way Mirrors, 159
Turnover in staff, 20

Understaffed, 10

Vacation Bible School, 78,79
Variety of methods, 132
Variety of programs, 88
Video cassettes, 106
Visitation, 78

Wednesday evening, 73,76
Women's groups, 77
Women's ministries, 44

Workshops for training, 118

Youth advisor, 42
Youth groups, 85
Youth involvement, 83
Youth methods, 138
Youth rooms, 149